How To Stay Married

Dick Hills

SUMMERSDALE

Copyright © Dick Hills 1995.

All rights reserved.

No part of this book may be reproduced by any means, nor transmitted, nor translated into a machine language, without the written permission of the publisher.

Summersdale Publishers
46 West Street
Chichester
West Sussex
PO19 1RP
England

A CIP catalogue record for this book is available from the British Library.

Printed and bound by Selwood Printing Ltd, Great Britain.

ISBN 1 873475 32 2

Original illustrations by Sophie Sitwell.

Contents

Prologue..4

Introduction..4

1. Sex before marriage (and after it)............................. 5
2. No confetti..12
3. Just cause 17
4. Mother-in-lawlessness...25
5. Can you keep a secret?...31
6. On picking one's own. 36
7. Water water everywhere..40
8. What every child knows about sex
   and the parents are afraid to ask............................45
9. How to stay married without living together............51
10. Don't die on a Friday..59
11. On the advantages of being nagged.......................64
12. Spare the rod and spoil your retirement.................68
13. An eye for the birds...74
14. What's in a name?..78
15. Fringe benefits from the birth of Jesus...................83
16. Pulling out all the plugs......................................90
17. All thy worldly goods..93
18. The re-patter of tiny feet...................................101
19. The keeper of the purse.....................................105
20. On getting lost...112
21. Keeping up with the Joneses...............................118
22. Spanish according to Mr. Doust...........................122
23. Coping with Anno Domini..................................127
24. The old dog and bone..132
25. Madness..141
26. The night they invented sex................................147
27. Residual guides to married life............................154

Epilogue
What sort of marriage would sir and madam prefer?......156

Prologue

Very few people have ever read Prologues so I haven't written one.

Dick Hills

Introduction

Very few people read Introductions either but it doesn't really matter.

How To Stay Married? That doesn't seem to be the modern problem. How to persuade people to get married is the present dilemma.

It's the modern practice for the girl and her 'live-in' boyfriend to rent a flat, hire a television set, and bonk themselves into oblivion, happy in the knowledge that if the bonking turns out to be a case of a left hand screw trying to get into a right hand thread, they can wave goodbye without going through the blender of a divorce.

Only if an offspring arrives, with another one on the way, do they have to make the decision either to get married or buy a television licence.

Usually the television licence wins, because such are the laws of our land after 2000 years of Christianity, that possessing a television set without a licence carries a heavy fine, but possessing a family without a marriage licence carries no fine at all. (In fact, they pay *you*.)

Against such odds I surrender, and confine my hints to those who have taken the mystical step into matrimony.

1. Sex before marriage (and after it)

Rule 1
Whether you have already (or intend to) practise either, it's just as well you know exactly what sex is in scientific terms. Sex has its origins in primordial biology... if an organism became damaged it would seek union with another in order to create a new, healthy organism. This has led to an awful lot of damaged bishops seeking union with actresses; but it doesn't mean you have to go out and break a leg before intercourse. Thinking about it is often damaging enough.

Rule 2
If as a married man or woman your sexual relationship takes a plunge, take a regular mixture of Benzedrine and Valium. This makes you randy, but if you don't strike lucky you don't give a damn.

Rule 3
Sexual potency is at its peak somewhere between two dozen oysters and a jar of 'Delay Cream'.

Personal Case History
There was more than the usual number in the psychiatric ward of the *Anchor and Hope* last week because it was rumoured that the landlord was having an affair with the new barmaid and the vultures were gathering to see what scraps could be picked up.

'Stolen fruits always taste sweeter,' pronounced a mild-mannered sweet sherry in the corner; which gave rise to a snort from a pint of bitter leaning on the bar, who expressed the view that some people thought once married, the sexual fruit-bowl was always available on the dining room table to help yourself whenever you felt like it (so to speak), which assumption in his experience was far from the case.

'What did he say?' asked an elderly mutt and jeff whiskey and water.

'He said,' shouted his companion winking at us all, 'that he always has it on the dining room table.'

'That's the proper place for it,' replied the deaf one, 'but now we watch the telly a lot, we have it on our laps.'

'I'm not talking about food,' said the pint of bitter, 'I'm talking about having sex.'

'So am I,' retorted the other.

Without a chairman the debate veered all over the pond like a mechanical toy motor boat without a rudder.

'... do you remember those ghastly Dutch caps? My God! You needed five days' notice to get yourself ready...' '... no central heating in those days dear, you had to have it in bed or in front of the fire because everywhere else was freezing...' '... when they got bored they used to do it in risky places like on the top of buses or in the public library...' '... if you didn't use a condom you just hoped the wife's dates were right...'

Attention was restored when the gin and tonic gave her husband a cuff and said, 'You never told me you had sex before we were married.' Her husband grinned sheepishly and stage-whispered, 'I mean with you dear, of course. With you.' This made his good lady even more irate. 'You certainly didn't have sex with me before we were married. I was brought up properly. I didn't believe in sex before marriage then and I don't believe in it now. You'd better think again. It wasn't with me you had sex.'

'Well I certainly had sex with someone,' he said.

'It wasn't with me I can assure you,' she concluded with some satisfaction and she wondered why everybody laughed.

The popular view always seems to be that sex before

marriage can't be compared with sex after it; a Bacchanalian feast compared with a meal in a works canteen. Congreve likened the two to a pretty piece of dialogue followed by a very dull play. Free sex embraces the thrill of a challenge, the variety of the quarry, and the mystery of the outcome - all of which adds to the piquancy of the sexual pursuit. Whereas married sex to the contrary has no surprises and soon becomes a matter of routine. 'Monogamy' as the school boy howler puts it 'is doing the same thing over and over again until you get bored.'

I can assure all those who wish to stay married that this needn't be the case. 'Let me not to the marriage of true minds admit impediments...' wrote Bill the bard as a sonnet opener, and let not me either. There are enough impediments in the way of true love, and monotony isn't one of them: which carries me and any of my readers who are interested to the Park Chambers Hotel on 6th Avenue and 52nd Street in New York in the summer of my life, where my business partner and I had been ensconced some three months. Following this period of enforced celibacy, we had accumulated enough capital to bring our wives over for a flying visit, primarily to relieve our concupiscence.

'I suppose we ought to do something about getting some preventatives,' I observed. 'I'll try that drug store down the block and see what they've got.'

'Oh - let me know how you get on,' returned my companion.

It was a typical American drug store composed of a chemist shop and a food counter dispensing coffee and Danish pastry and milkshakes. A scattering of customers were lounging on stools. Over the next few minutes I experienced what it was like running full tilt into a language block. A polite assistant approached with a 'Yessir - can I help you?'

'Yes. Do you stock preventatives?'

'Sorry sir?'

'Preventatives. You know . . . preventatives?'

'Oh! You mean like for colds and flu. You want capsules or liquid? We have . . .'

'No I don't mean for colds. I mean - we call them Durex. Have you a packet of Durex?'

'Durex? I don't remember the brand. Hey Joe!' he called over to the soda jerk. 'Have you heard of Durex?'

"Have you heard of Durex?"

Joe shook his head. 'The gentleman's English, Nick. May be it's a different brand over here. Ask him what it is.'

'What is it exactly, sir?' Nick asked.

'Don't you call them French letters over here?' I asked. By this time the customers had become interested and swivelled round on their stools.

'Is that the brand name, French letters?' inquired Nick.

'Let me explain, you see, I haven't seen my wife for a long time and she's coming over this week.'

'That's great for you sir. She'll love New York, it's a wonderful town.'

'Yes I know it is, but . . .'

'Don't forget to take her to the Rockefeller Center,' called out a male customer, 'There's a noo exhibition there this week.'

'Thanks,' I called.

'Shall I fetch the manager sir?' Nick suggested.

'No, I don't need the manager,' I said in desperation, 'I need - you know - a preventative to wear for the wife . . .'

'Oh! You mean RUBBERS sir! I gotcha.'

The customers gave us a round of applause.

I need hardly add at this point that the word condom had scarcely been invented let alone passed into universal usage at the time, and that the American word 'rubbers' was entirely new to me. Being American made, the smallest pack the assistant produced was the size of a small shoe-box, which I could hardly refuse after his services, and cost me twelve dollars.

'Have a nice day,' said Nick as he presented me with the wrapped bulk.

'With these I could have a nice year.' I said.

Several days went by and the time came to re-arrange our rooms in the hotel to accommodate our wishes, as my colleague and I had been sharing a suite.

'By the way, how did you get on at the drug store? I'd

better fit myself out.' I related the whole incident while he dissolved into fits of laughter.

'So what do they call them here?' he asked at length. I can say that in all honesty the word 'rubbers' completely escaped me. It was such an odd usage it refused to come back. I agonised to recall it.

'It doesn't matter anyway,' he said, 'I'll get Sam to get them for me.'

Sam was the elderly hotel bell-hop and a typical New York fixer. For a dollar tip he could fetch you anything. ('Any time you guys want a couple of broads let me know'). For our entertainment he gave us a running commentary on all the dudes in the hotel, who was sleeping with whom, and what scams were going on. Over the months of our prolonged stay he had become our bosom pal and confidante. My friend called down for him and he duly arrived.

'Sam,' opened up my companion, 'can you get me a packet of preventatives, I think they're about twelve dollars.' He counted out some bills.

'Sure Mr Baker,' said Sam. 'You got a cold coming on? It's the air conditioning.'

'Not for colds, I mean Durex, French letters.'

'Sorry sir?'

'He knows the right name,' said my friend pointing at me accusingly, 'but he says he can't remember it. You see - my wife is coming over for a few days -'

'Oh, I'm happy to hear that. She'll love New York.'

'Yes, I know she will but . . .'

'Don't forget to take her to the Rockefeller Center . . .'

'I know, there's a new exhibition there,' interrupted the other. By now I was starting to giggle.

'You did this deliberately!' said my frustrated friend. 'You don't understand Sam, my wife is coming over. We haven't seen each other for a long time, as well you know, and we love each other very much.'

'I guess you must. You two guys are the talk of the hotel the way you behave yourselves.'

'We love each other very much and we want to do what husbands and wives always do,' pursued my friend. I was lying on the bed with tears of silent mirth in my eyes. He was on the point of physically giving a demonstration of the act when as bad luck would have it Sam cottoned on.

'You want some rubbers sir?'

'That's the word!' I spluttered.

'Well get some of those Sam.'

'Hold it!' I suddenly realised. 'What are we bothering for?' I grabbed my own packet. 'There's a thousand of them in this packet. You can take half of these. I forgot all about it.' My room-mate threw me a disgusted look. From that day to this he is still convinced that I knew they were called 'rubbers'.

If nothing else, perhaps this incident records for posterity a moment in the history of sex, for it would never have arisen without some lingering gentility even among men. I'm sure in these days when folk are more brutally direct, our needs could have been lucidly expressed in four words.

Helpful Hint

Don't underestimate the power of sex. It has brought down governments. It brought down Ted Heath and Margaret Thatcher, in my view, because neither appeared to have any.

2. No Confetti?

Rule 1
This subject brings us to the church and your intended bride. Marry a plain girl rather than a beautiful one. When a woman's beauty fades with age she invariably blames it on her life with you. A plain girl, however, has nothing to fear from the advancing years.

But don't let her spend £50 on a perm: for that money the perm deserves a better face!

Rule 2
Before saying 'I do', be wary of, and make allowances for, religious differences. (His religion might be Manchester United, and hers the Argos catalogue.) Also remember that for Jews, circumcision has a deeper religious significance, but for Gentiles it is just a way of getting rid of dick heads... See Shakespeare 'There is a divinity that shapes our ends, rough hewn though it be.'

Rule 3
Compatibility in your pursuits, outlook and interests is more important than sexual attraction, and it takes time to acquire assurance. However, if you're short of time, a quick compatibility test is to stare fixedly at her breasts for five minutes, and if her nipples stand up, it means you're in with a chance.

Personal Case History
A very influential critic, reading my rough notes on the snares and pitfalls encountered by those who wish to stay married, expressed the opinion that my advice was outdated and

irrelevant to the lifestyles of modern marriages. Normally I pay no attention to the critics, but this particular critic happens to cook my food, iron my shirts, bear my children and weed my garden. Ignoring her comments can sometimes result in a week long loaded silence signifying inner pain, for which not even an apology is an abirritant. So, dutifully I reread my notes to see if I had allowed the odd neolithic slip to show beneath the skirts of my observations. I detected none. I hadn't once called the movies 'the pictures', the radio 'the wireless', or referred to a dress as a 'frock'. I resisted the temptation at one time to allude to Glenda Farrell and Barton McClaine movies in case it dated me. I pointed this out to the duchess.

'You used the word *confetti*,' she sniffed. 'That dates you. Half the married kids today have never heard of confetti. Most churches banned it years ago.' I gazed at her hollow-eyed and disbelieving in much the same way that Queen Isabel must have looked at Columbus when he told her the world was round. 'No confetti!' I croaked. 'There must be. It was a clue in *The Times* yesterday.'

'What young couples read *The Times*?' she rejoined. 'You prattle on about marriage but when did you last go to a wedding?'

'I went to ours,' I said defensively.

'Only just,' she reminded me. 'Your body turned up but the rest of you was lying on the floor at the *Anchor and Hope* where you left it the night before.' Then she gave me a peck. 'Still, I'm glad you made it. But my advice is to go to a wedding and bring your advice up to date. If you can find one. Half the couples these days don't bother with marriage at all.'

Statistics of course prove the duchess to be right, although to judge from the scene at our local church the following Saturday, the opposite was the case. There were three weddings all going on at once; one wedding coming out and two queuing up to go in. One Best Man was going berserk because his photographer was taking pictures of the wrong wedding. I soon discovered that a wedding party today falls into two groups. There is the mums-and-dads group who wear dresses and hats and suits with carnations. And then there are the others who wear anything as long as it doesn't look like a dress or a suit. The groom emerged from the church wearing a sort of oatmeal safari jacket and the bride was wearing a more eccentric version of the gear Barbra Streisand wears when passing through London Airport on her way to Paris.

'Oo she's beautiful,' sighed a highly painted nymph, who looked as though she'd quickly tarted up after cutting a lesson at Grange Hill School. 'Crinkled cotton!' The crinkled cotton explained why the bride looked as though she'd spent all night in the wedding car; an effect I'm sure she strove to achieve.

I groped my way into the church hoping to find that I wasn't on Mars after all but on the earth I knew and loved. No hushed voices inside whispering against the muted tones of the church organ. It was more like a rehearsal of a television show. Video cameras were being aimed, flash cameras blinked everywhere. Noise and laughter. I staggered into a pew and grasped a copy of the wedding service. Ah! That was better. Hymn 520 . . . 'Love divine all loves excelling. Joy in heaven on earth come down.' So we were on earth after all! A good old traditional English hymn. I stood up, diaphragm pumped up ready to belt out the familiar tune. My mouth was already open when a scruffy pop group leapt to its feet, plucked guitars and launched into a rendering of Hymn 520 which sounded more like *Hey Jude*. I stared around aghast. Nobody seemed to mind. A few old ladies started to swing their frames in a mild disco style and smile at each other as they sang, in the way that old people do. The stained glass window above the altar started to whirl slowly round and round . . .

How To Stay Married 15

"Hey Jude, don't make it bad..."

I can hardly remember the wedding service. I knew that it was supposed to start with something like 'Dearly beloved, we are gathered here in the sight of God . . .' but I can't remember God being mentioned at all. Maybe he decided not to turn up, and I don't blame him. I learned afterwards at the reception, my shock further unstrung by cheap sherry, that couples today can dictate more or less what they want to be contained in the marriage vows. To judge from the present divorce rate, the favourite seems to be, 'for richer for poorer, for better for worse, but not for long.'

I weaved my way home and collapsed into my favourite chair.

'So what do you think?' asked the duchess. 'Did you learn anything?'

'I don't know,' I mumbled, 'if weddings aren't so popular these days, it's probably because the parents talk them out of having them. I know I would.'

'But what about the confetti?'

'Confetti?' I murmured. 'What's confetti?'

Helpful Hint

Confetti is messy, and gets everywhere. It has the nasty habit, when in the final throes of orgasm, of dropping out of your ears on to your beloved's face. Seek the vicar's sanction to have rice thrown: your bride might turn a little peckish during the act.

3. Just cause...

Rule 1

The shortest marriage on record began: 'We had a happy marriage but then on the way to the reception...'

Do not subscribe to the usual weak reasons offered as a 'Just cause' for divorce...

'When I asked my new wife why her mother had cried throughout the wedding she said, 'look in a mirror.''

'My wife lied about her age. She'll never live to be as old as she looks.'

'I just hate the way my husband keeps smiling in his sleep.'

'She kept calling herself Olympic Torch because she says she never goes out.'

'I consented to an arranged marriage because they said my intended had a face like Helen of Troy - the face that launched a thousand ships. I couldn't say no because they were right - she had a face like a Champagne bottle.'

Rule 2

A worthy quote from a reader who has been happily married for sixty years: 'from the beginning my wife and I agreed to share the decisions. She decides when I can go out and when I can't and what money I can spend, but leaves me to decide what to do about the Middle East situation.' Fairness triumphs in the end.

Rule 3

If ever your wife complains that she married beneath her, quote to her that ancient proverb, 'The patch on the arse of a man's trousers is not necessarily the window to his soul.'

Personal Case History

We had just repaired to the psychiatric ward of the *Anchor and Hope* after the drink had run out at the reception of a local wedding.

'That bit about "if any man can show just cause why these two shall not be joined together",' asked a pint of real ale. 'D'you think that anyone ever stands up and objects?'

'Only in American movies,' said a pink gin.

'I wish someone had stood up and objected at my wedding,' muttered a whiskey and soda, a well known loser on the race track. 'But it's only a formality isn't it? Unless you happen to know the groom is a rapist or murderer, or worse still, a bookie!'

'But it doesn't actually define what *just cause* is, does it? pursued the real ale. 'What would happen if the bride's mother stood up and said "Yes I object on the grounds that the groom is an idle layabout and a drunk"?'

'It would wipe out ninety per cent of weddings,' I answered. 'The snag with the challenge being made in the wedding ceremony is that you don't really find a just cause for not being joined together until after you've been joined together. It's a bit like the journey of Theseus - you don't meet up with the monsters until you're well on your way.'

'I would have paid somebody to stand up and object at my wedding,' put in the pink gin, 'if I had known Gladys spent money like water. She's no will power whatsoever. And what I mean by will power is being able to go into a supermarket to buy a tin of cocoa and come out with only a tin of cocoa.' For a while the group indulged in an orgy of *if onlys* '... if only I had known my wife was going to leave her libido in the vestry ... turn into a house proud fanatic ... love sauerkraut and garlic in everything ... invite her mother round every Sunday ... wear a two-way stretch bra over four-way fat ... etc.'

'How about you?' asked the real ale, eyeing me over the

rim of his glass. 'The preternatural married man, the epitome of epithalamium, a golden wedding coming up. Can you think of a just cause at this late hour?'

This wasn't a fair question to ask a coward like me. Maybe cowardice was the secret of my success?

'Well come on old boy,' boomed he. 'It surely can't be a case of *amor vincit omnia*?'

'Well, if I had known what I know now,' I ventured, 'I would have added a clause to the marriage vows about Australian t.v. soaps.'

The duchess is wont, in the middle of anything, to excuse herself hurriedly - 'My programme's on' - *My programme* is a generic expression she uses to describe any one of a dozen Australian soap operas to which in later life she has become addicted. The reason is, I think, that in my later life, I wasn't so much the disgusting cad I used to be, and consequently her life has become much duller and she supplements the lack of excitement with a daily dose of soap.

As soon as she switches on I scurry hollow-eyed from the room and look around desperately for something to do until the ritual is over. It has to be confessed, we have reached a stage of television divorce.

It all began several years ago when we bought our first V.C.R. set. Our Simon had just reached that age when he was at pains to prove that, technologically, his mother and I were dinosaurs and that we should buy the latest model which displayed more buttons than the control panel of Concorde.

'On this set,' he demonstrated, 'you can record nine hours of television in one programme setting. And up to a month ahead.'

'But we don't know what is on television a month ahead,' I objected. 'I doubt very much if even the BBC and ITV know what will be on a month ahead. In fact, since your mother cancelled the *Radio Times* because she said it was too expensive for a lot of rubbish, *we* don't even know what's on a week ahead. And as for recording nine hours of television, I would find it very difficult finding nine hours of television worth recording.'

'Look, you know *Coronation Street* always comes on at a certain time. You could record the series while you were away on holiday.'

'Oh, that's a good idea,' said the duchess. I realised at that point that our harmonious passions and tastes were beginning to show a parting of ways.

During the ensuing months our conjugal knot slackened noticeably as I struggled and failed miserably with the machine of a thousand buttons. If it had been Concorde I would have crashed it before taking off. At first the duchess ascribed my errors charitably to thick fingers. 'You must be pressing two buttons at once. You've just recorded an hour of Channel 24 and we haven't got a Channel 24.'

A major crisis occurred when, on an injunction to record an hour and a half on the Royal Family, I captured half an hour of *Tomorrow's World* and an hour on the paintings of the Pre-Raphaelites. The duchess' howls of anguish could be heard three doors away, so our neighbours attest. Thereafter, whatever I recorded I seemed to get Wogan. There was always the odd button I seemed to miss - or was it those thick fingers again?

I had my own machine taken away from me in the end! The duchess pinched the remote control and hid it until she needed it.

And then one evening entertaining friends, we found ourselves discussing movies old and new.

'There's a brilliant oldie coming up next week,' commented an enthusiast. 'Don't miss it if you haven't seen it, it's called *The Killing* with Sterling Hayden. I won't give it away now but it's got a sensational ending. Basically it's about a race track robbery where you end up - you know - actually hoping they will get away with it. But you'd never guess the twist at the end . . .'

Seven days later the telephone rang. It was the duchess staying overnight baby-sitting for our eldest. 'Don't forget to record *The Killing*. Make sure the clock on the video is the right time. Don't use your fingers, use a pen or something. Make sure you've got the right channel and the right time, and if it's the BBC don't forget to record more time because they're always late. And make sure it bleeps properly when you lock it in.'

'Never mind all that,' I said, annoyed at being treated like a six year old, which I was with that machine, 'where is the remote control hidden?'

There was only the briefest of pauses before she said, 'under the custard creams in the biscuit tin. Try not to mess it up dear. I've invited Ken and Rose round to watch it with us and have supper.'

In due course, the four of us sat spellbound as we watched Sterling stagger into the airport with his girl on one arm and a bulging suitcase full of stolen dollars under the other. We quivered in suspense when the airline clerk won the argument to have the suitcase put into the baggage hold, knowing the big twist at the end was nigh, and . . . and then . . . Sterling Hayden and his girl dissolved into a blinking screen of black and white dots . . .

The silence that followed is still going on in a way. The one instruction I had forgotten (and there was always one) was that of recording for extra time because of the BBC's habit of always running late. I don't think it provided the duchess with the *just cause* why we should no longer be joined together, but over the next twenty four hours I would rather have been caught naked in bed with another woman or jabbing heroin into my arm with a syringe.

While the scars were healing, Australian soaps arrived on the scene. A tradition had been established of our always viewing together and sinking our separate tastes in the great cause of togetherness. I would sit dry-eyed through a June Allyson weepy while the duchess got through a box of Kleenex; and she crocheted her way stonily through a Lee Marvin action movie or ten frames of snooker as a quid pro quo.

Australian soaps brought an end to all that and the duchess got ratty every time I headed for the door.

'*Neighbours* is very big in Australia,' she said defensively. 'Praise comes from no lower down,' I said.

I tried to like them. I really did. But it is very difficult getting hooked on a drama which has a surprise party for Wayne and Maureen as its highest peak. After watching a few episodes I began to count the number of times one of the characters said, 'I want to apologise about last night'. Doctors apologised to nurses, cleaners apologised to store owners, sexy broads apologised to uncles, young people apologised to each other, all about what happened last night. I thought Australia must be one hell of a place at night.

I said to the duchess, 'When did anybody apologise to you about anything? In real life nobody apologises except for little things that don't matter. If they do the dirty on you they go into hiding and don't speak to you any more.' After a time I recognised it as the scriptwriter's device for bringing two characters together in Scene 5 Page 29, who would normally be miles apart.

'Hallo Wayne! What are yew dooin' heere? Shouldn't yes bee ett the sergury?'

'Yea. Bit I cawled een cos I wanted to apologise about larst night.'

'Yea - I rickin yew ort to - callin' me a whore in front of orl my freens.'

'Aw c'mon Maureen! Put it down to jealousy. Let me mek it up to yew. Come out 'n hev dinner with me tonight.'

Maureen does of course go out to dinner with Wayne (because they are both contracted for another twenty episodes) and bump into Wayne's old school-mate Doreen, who calls Maureen a cradle-snatcher, but that's O.K. because next day she calls on Maureen and says 'I want to apologise about last night' and this enables them to become bosom pals when otherwise they would have nothing more to do with each other; and naturally Doreen then steals Wayne away from Maureen and there is a hell of a love triangle bust-up for six weeks when they're all going to kill each other, until the scriptwriter realises there is another series coming up and so he gets all three to apologise to each other.

You could, in fact, take an episode out of one soap and insert it into another and nobody would notice the difference.

By that time my forbearance came under heavy strain and I found myself looking for a bolt-hole as soon as those twangy accents boomed around the lounge walls. It might be a bit odd to confess that such cracks that have appeared in our married path to golden glory have not been caused by infidelity, desertion, or brutality, but by spools of video-tape flown over from Sidney and Adelaide. Hopefully all will be well once I have apologised to the duchess about last night. (I taped a profile of Neil Kinnock in mistake for *The Golden Girls*.) Meanwhile if you know the ending of *The Killing* keep it to yourself.

Helpful Hint
Watching television has only one advantage over the cinema ... it's not so far from the toilet.

4. Mother-in-lawlessness

Rule 1
It is said in legend that a witch can only cry three tears, and those out of the left eye. Watch your mother-in-law closely at the wedding.

Rule 2
Noah was busy naming the animals as each pair ascended into the Ark. Two vicious tusked creatures, snorting and snarling, appeared up the ramp.

'I name thee . . . warthogs,' pronounced Noah.

'Why did you pick that name?' asked Mrs. Noah. Noah shrugged.

'Because they look a bit like your mother,' he said.

But Rule 2 should stress the need to stay off the jokes. Don't forget she is your future baby-sitter.

Rule 3
Don't take expensive colour snaps of the wife's mother - they might all come out.

Personal Case History
'Did you hear about poor old Charlie? He got copped for committing bigamy.'

'Bigamy eh? Did he get a heavy sentence?'

'The worst - two mothers-in-law.'

Yes, we're all familiar with mother-in-law jokes, the last refuge of the costive comic. The archetypal ma-in-law within this tradition is depicted as a rigid woman without one soft point of feminine weakness. She is always in the right, totally devoid of a sense of humour, an inveterate meddler in her offsprings' marital affairs, convinced that her daughter married beneath her, and that her son-in-law is an idle waster. She is prone to come for the weekend and stay for a fortnight.

All this is a travesty of the truth: there must be at least half a dozen mothers-in-law somewhere in the world who are not like that.

My own mother-in-law, the Grand Duchess, is hardly a Mother of the Gracchi, but she did come for a weekend and stay for forty years. In fact she stayed until she died at 90 and went to that great son-in-law's mansion in the sky. I admit that this does expose me as the world's greatest wimp, but it didn't happen quite like that. I refer to the conversation at the time she became a widow, which unfortunately occurred as we moved into our first house.

'I can't really leave her on her own,' the duchess said appealingly, and I agreed with her, because I thought she meant that she was going to find someone else to live with her. By the time this misunderstanding was sorted out, it was too late, and I was clearing out the spare room. (Warning to newly-weds, don't get a house with a spare room.)

What possessed the duchess, normally as rational as a convention of Socratean Guardians, to introduce this high-risk factor into our family life? It wasn't as if we lived in a castle and could dump the Grand Duchess in the East wing and wave to her now and again as we went past in the Roller. We had a three-up and two-down. The answer to this riddle is found in the family history.

The grand duchess was born in Riga, Latvia, and there she was in the early 'twenties, a gay young thing, walking up and down Riga and waiting for Mr. Right to come along, which is what they did in the 'twenties quite a lot. Mr. Right turned up in the shape of Ralph Edgar Warren, reputed to be the youngest Royal Marine ever when he was inducted into the service as an orphan, and now batman to Lord Alexander, attending to his Lordship during a goodwill visit to the Baltic States.

Following the marriage, Ralph Edgar was forced to deposit his new bride in London and return to the ocean wave. There she pined away, like Ruth amid the alien corn, absolutely alone, a foreigner in a strange land.

'She couldn't speak a word of English you know,' confided the duchess, the suspicion of a sentimental tear moistening her Shandian lashes. My admiration went out to Ralph Edgar, who, without a single word of Lettish to his name, had somehow swept a foreign maiden off her feet by sign language.

'She had nothing to do, so she spent all her time at the pictures, that's how she learned her English,' added the duchess. I concluded that English must be the easiest language in the world to learn. Is that its hidden secret? Given the reverse, I could have watched Latvian movies for a thousand years and not picked up the lingo. Besides, if that *was* the way she learned English, she would have had an American accent, because all the movies at that time had Joan Blondell and Jimmy Cagney in them. I didn't quite buy that one. In fact, even after fifty years, the Grand Duchess had a European accent you could cut with a rolling pin and sounded like a cross between Zsa Zsa Gabor and S.Z. 'Cuddles' Sackall.

'I spoke fluent Russian as a child,' continued the duchess. 'I'll never quite forgive my mother for not keeping it up with me. I could have got myself a wonderful job.'

Job or no job, I was glad her mother didn't. Apart from being nagged in two languages, I don't think I could have borne the burden of over forty years of prolonged exchanges between my wife and mother-in-law in a foreign tongue. My sympathies went out to Queen Victoria, who had all that trouble with her polyglot family.

'If your mother is Latvian,' I countered, 'how is it that she never speaks Lettish but speaks German?'

'Ah that's because all her family came from Germany,

and after the first war they were given the choice of staying in Germany or going to Russia, and her family went to Latvia.' The long silence that followed measured my confusion. I gave up. There is no explaining the migratory habits of the continentals. After a thousand wars and an equal number of years of refugeeism, they got into the habit of changing nationalities regularly. And so in due time the Grand Duchess turned up with her crucifix, her cherished pieces of furniture which included an upright piano, her family album, and a titanium-wrought resilience to misfortune which her mid-European stock had bequeathed.

'What, no budgerigar?' I declared.

'Is dat von of Dick's funny chokes?' enquired the good lady of the duchess. Well I was testing her. After all, she had come to live with us and I wanted to know where the boundaries lay.

'Now according to your family history,' I put to her later, later being about 1955, 'two of your brothers are German, so during the last war, they were in the Werhmacht!' The Grand Duchess shrugged.

'Dots how it vos,' she said. Dots how it vos. All par for the course.

'Now supposing they had been drafted into the Luftwaffe,' I mused. 'When you were bombed out during the London blitz, they might well have been the two who dropped the bomb on you!'

'Is dot anodder von of your chokes?' she asked. It wasn't as if she had no sense of humour, it simply wasn't an English one. I don't know what the Latvians laugh at. The Grand Duchess laughed quite a lot but not at jokes (she stared at Hancock shows po-faced). She laughed mainly in conversation and in company. Her laugh was the sort of gay tinkling laugh accompanied by a coy fluttering of the hand that Mahler's heroines emit in between choruses in the ballroom scenes. One could almost imagine a fan in her other hand.

In fact, the more I became familiar with her ways the more I was overwhelmed with the awesome impression she was cocooned in the continental provincial life of the twenties and thrust amongst us as if in a time-warp. She seemed oblivious of current events, she established no independent life of her own, even though she was relatively young in years. She gradually repudiated her friends and relations, and the only meaning she gained from life was through her daughter.

Now we begin to see the strands of a plot coming together. Was the duchess only too aware of her mother's reclusive nature? Is this why she uttered 'I can't really leave her on her own'? Was her prudence weakened by compassion at the prospect of her mother, an abandoned alien as a bride, again suffering loneliness as an abandoned widow? Ah! Such drama! What if I had objected, or postured with 'It's either her or me!'. On what fragile supports stands the Hymeneal altar!

The duchess fondly imagined when we moved to a larger house that her mother would retire to her bed-sit for most of the day and knit and watch television and join us for meals; but the grand lady refused such a life and continued to live in the bosom of the family. She gyrated in a tight orbit round her daughter. The duchess became incensed at her not allowing us an hour or two's privacy in the evening, remaining rooted to her chair until the pictures flickered off the t.v. screen. For all that she was a handy baby-sitter, a walker of the dog, a demon gardener, and an amusing assassin of the English language: among her choice expressions were 'bread and droopins', 'sharp as a noodle', 'as black as new dicks knockers', and 'who d'you tink I am - head book and cocklewasher?', it was the duchess more than I who lived to regret her fatal decision.

O ye betrothed who burn to be wed
Far from thy mothers settle thy bed!

Perhaps that is the only piece of sound advice for married tyros. Uncle Penstemon's warning to Mr. Polly on the subject of wives ('you don't know what you've got until you take 'em home and unwrap 'em') might equally apply to mothers-in-law; it's a lottery as to whether you get a good'un or a bad'un and there are no rules about it. Do all women become like their mothers? Surely not. Only just lately . . .

Helpful Hint

A wise man seeks the favour of his in-laws, for in the wars of the wedded only fools will spurn an ally.

5. Can You Keep a Secret?

Rule 1
The general rule whenever a friend or neighbour asks you if you can keep a secret is to say 'No I can't' because they are going to tell you anyway, and you can always blame it on them if the secret gets out. Play each secret by ear. If it is whispered that the couples in Nos. 34 and 38 are running wife-swapping parties, you might decide to spread that around, in the hope of swapping your wife for a lawn-mower.

Rule 2
An estate agent was describing the wonderful amenities of the area to a couple of prospective house-buyers. 'I must admit however,' he wound up, 'it's a shocking neighbourhood for gossip!' 'Did you hear that dear?' said the wife eagerly. 'And you've got your garden!' Count the gossip value as a plus factor. It will keep the wife's mind off your own secrets.

Rule 3
Which leads us to the third rule; never, never, never, keep secrets from your wife; she will always find them out in the end. But try your hardest.

Personal Case History
Customarily, after my return from work, the duchess keeps me abreast of local goings-on.

'I ran into Peggy Cartwright this afternoon,' she opened up one evening over her crochet work. 'Keep it under your hat, but apparently Diedre and Nigel have broken up . . .'

(The definition of *apparently* in this context is: *according to unproved but generally reliable gossip.*

'They are living together for the time being,' the duchess

pursued, 'because they don't want anybody to know until they decide what to do.'

'How many other people have been told to keep it under their hats apart from us and the whole neighbourhood?' I asked.

'You know what I mean. Don't go putting your foot in it at any sort of get-together. As far as they are concerned nobody knows about it.'

'If you hadn't told me, I wouldn't have put my foot in it because I wouldn't have known about it,' I observed.

'I only told you to warn you,' sniffed the crochet worker. 'In case you said something accidentally.'

I lapsed into silence. Married conversations often whirl round in illogical circles of this kind. But there's something illogical about secrets anyway. If a person keeps a secret, it doesn't really exist, because nobody knows there is a secret. The only secrets that are manifest are those which are blabbed all over town. In any case, do you know anyone in the world who, when a friend whispers 'Can you keep a secret?', screams 'No I can't! I'm a blabber mouth! Don't tell me!' He'd be ostracised like a monkey who refused mutual grooming. We are obliged to say 'Yes' just to reaffirm our membership of the local tribe.

In fact, the imparting of secrets is a good way to test your status in the integrity pecking order. The 'first to know' are those at sump level, the inveterate gossips and nosey-parkers like Peggy Cartwright, with the ethics of a warthog and the mischievous tautophony of the village parrot. If you are almost last on the list to be told, it means at least that your probity and integrity are intact.

But let's all be honest and admit that 'keeping' secrets is the quickest way of disseminating gossip. Even when we were kids at school it was the secrets we remembered more than the lessons.

'And what did you learn at school today, Penny?'

'Freddie Peabody wets the bed. Ha ha! . . .'

The body politic is honeycombed with this childish frailty. Government departments spring more leaks than a French plumbing system. As soon as we are privy to some restricted information, we have a burning desire to tell somebody. I feel sorry for spies and high-ranking officials who know the position of all our Polaris submarines, the password into our missile bases, and the sexual deviations of the Chinese General Chief of Staff, and can't tell a soul. They must spend every night in their bedrooms banging their heads against the wall.

It wasn't surprising that during the 70's and 80's the great powers started to swap secrets, the stuff that Frederick Forsyth's novels were made on. They couldn't keep it to themselves any longer. The Russians and the Americans swapped a secret, and the catharsis not being absolute, the Russians then offered to swap their American secret for a British secret.

'Vot have you got to swap?'

'We have a very interesting titbit about our Minister of Defence Freddie Peabody . . .'

'Vot is that?'

'He still wets the bed. Ha ha!'

The fateful evening came round when the duchess and I were at a social gathering which included the fractured pair: Diedre and Nigel - which nobody was supposed to know about but everybody did, and pretended they didn't. Diedre and Nigel meanwhile, played their parts perfectly of a happily married couple who were looking forward to their silver and golden anniversaries, because they thought that nobody knew about their separating and were intent on behaving as if they weren't. At least that was what we had been *told* they thought!

'We'd better chat with them,' hissed the duchess, warningly. 'We don't want them to suspect anything.'

'Don't blame me if I make a mistake,' I hissed back. 'Because I'm finding it very difficult to sort out in my mind what I would say if I were ignorant of the bust up, and what I would say if I knew about the bust up and was pretending I didn't!'

'The same thing,' advised the duchess, switching to a smile as we approached Diedre and Nigel. For some reason my knees began to tremble. Well there was a reason. Women are very good at this sort of dissimulation. Congreve wrote a whole bunch of plays on the subject. In contrast, I am like a twit with neon lights flashing on my forehead. Darting through my mind was the last occasion when I was asked to keep the secret that Ness Hutchins was both unmarried and pregnant, and my opening innocent but unacceptable remark was, 'Hallo Ness. You've put on a bit of weight, haven't you?'

Fortunately our opening chat with Diedre and Nigel went along harmless lines. Nigel asked if my back injury had patched up and Diedre asked how the children were getting along. The atmosphere became relaxed, and we chatted freely as we did in the old days.

'So,' I beamed at Nigel, 'where are you going for your holidays this year?'

This earned me a kick in the shins from the duchess. Somebody else interrupted, and my wife pulled me aside.

'Why did you ask that? You *know* they can't be going on holiday together.'

'No I don't,' I protested, the Plymouth gin and dry martini not yet having taken charge of my tongue. 'I don't *know* about their bust up, remember?'

'But asking questions like that makes out that you do, and that you're deliberately baiting them to come out with it.'

Frankly at this point I gave up. The attitudinising had become so sophisticated I would defy even Congreve to absorb it. But before I could think up another word Nigel said,

'You were asking about our holidays. The fact is that Diedre and I have decided to separate, didn't anybody tell you that?'

The few seconds of silence that followed could have been borrowed from outer space . . .

As it turned out, Diedre and Nigel had told Peggy Cartwright about their separation, certain in the knowledge that it would be common knowledge within twenty four hours, which it was, except that nobody would confess to it because it was a *secret*.

'It's just as well,' said the duchess the following evening. 'If it had been a secret, you were the one who would have blown it.'

'I know,' I sighed. 'Subconsciously I suppose, I don't like the idea of a group of people nursing a secret about somebody just for the pleasure of it, and my impulse is to blow the gaff. Death to all the Peggy Cartwrights.'

The duchess snorted.

'Peggy Cartwright! I know a few things about her. Can you keep a secret?'

'Of course!' I replied, leaning forward eagerly.

Helpful Hint

How to turn any woman into your slave: pretend you know a secret about her friend which you'll tell her some day.

6. On picking one's own

Rule 1

Modern living accentuates the multiplicity of choice, so make the most of the options open to you as a married couple. In contraceptive methods there are the pill, the condom, the Dutch cap the coil and the holding the breath. The latter method is only used when you realise you have forgotten to use any of the others.

For married couples with kids, leave your bedroom door open and practise *coitus interruptus*.

If you choose to be undisturbed however, a useful sex-aid is Vaseline. Smarm plenty on your bedroom door knob.

The *rhythm method* can lead to embarrassments. What husband wants to be in the middle of a rugby scrum when the wife runs onto the pitch with a thermometer in her mouth and a calendar in her hand shouting 'It's *now* Charlie!'?

Rule 2

'You know what the foolproof contraceptive is?' asked the doctor of a nubile lass.

'No.'

'You've got it.'

Rule 3

You can either marry or not. The choice is yours. If your marriage fails, don't blame the institution. That's like wanting to do away with the Grand National because your horse fell at a fence. Men whose wives become lazy often make their secretaries their mistresses. Again the choice is yours and the consequences . . . Your secretary will get a little behind at work and your wife will get a big one at home. You can either marry someone your own age, or someone three times your age . . . provided you're willing to accept the urge difference.

Personal Case History

I was lying in bed last Sunday morning and minding my own business, when the duchess observed as she turned the page of her newspaper,

'I see you can pick your own now.'

I should warn all young people who are trying to stay married that wives are prone to uttering random reflections upon their newspaper garnerings. It's a sort of test. If the marriage is still working the husband is expected to respond with a touch of warm interest 'What's that dear?' Be prepared for almost anything. The usual comments are: 'I knew there was something funny about that business . . .' or 'I see he didn't get away with it in the end . . .' or simply 'God - would you credit it?'

Being an old hand I usually allow myself a few idle speculations (internal of course) before asking the obligatory question. 'I see you can pick your own now' might for example refer to my Uncle Arthur's habit; he has been picking his own for years. Would the world be better, I ask myself, if our bad habits were given official sanction? Having reared a bunch of kids, I wonder if teenage problems would disappear if it were made official that they didn't have to wash?

On the other hand, 'I see that you can pick your own now' might allude to some daring horticultural experiment, with the appropriate message chalked on the side of the road. 'P. Y. O. orchids. 200 yds on left.'

It doesn't pay to dwell too long on personal whimsies.

'Pick your own what dear?'

'The sex of your child. According to these genetic engineers, or whatever, couples will be able to pick a boy or a girl. I don't think I would like that, would you?'

'Absolutely not!'

(I've been married too long to the duchess to disagree. In *young* married homes, every subject debated is a Private Member's Bill - you can vote how you want. By the time the last of the confetti is swept out of the house, all household debates must be voted on according to the party line.)

It so happened that on this occasion I agreed with the duchess, although not for the same reasons. Being responsible for the actual sex of one's brood would only make husbands more vulnerable. Take the typical example of returning home from work and finding her in one of those moods over the kids.

'Don't sit down. I want you to have a word with your daughter!' (They are always yours when there's trouble.)

The prisoner at the bar - five years old with big innocent eyes - has tipped the sugar bowl over the new V.C.R. set. The jury consisting of one good woman and true, has found her guilty, and has now called upon you as judge to pronounce sentence and administer punishment.

Don't try all that nonsense about hearing the prisoner's side of the story. You'll be charged as an accessory and sentenced with the criminal. Throw the book at the nasty left-wing terrorist and your future in the Party is assured. Just be thankful that no blame can be attached to you.

After all, you didn't pick on having a daughter. She was the result of a purely random concatenation of hormones. It could have been an angelic little boy, but instead you got this scruffy little villain.

Now just consider how much more culpable you would have been if the choice of the sex had been left to you. Son or daughter? And you had picked a daughter! Or worse still, you had an argument about the sex and you had won. The recriminations would have been endless. . .

'*You* chose to have a daughter! You talk to her . . .'

'If we'd had a boy - as I wanted - we wouldn't have had all this trouble!'

'Pity you didn't think of the wedding when you chose to have a daughter. Now you're complaining about the cost!'

It's not up to me to advise young couples what they should do when this marvel of sex-determination is introduced. Personally, I would leave the choice to God. At least He would have to share the blame when sugar bowls are tipped over new V.C.R. sets.

Helpful Hints

It is now possible for expectant parents to be told the sex of the child before its actual birth. Since the sex will remain unchanged whether it is heard on the 6 or the 9 o'clock news, it would appear to serve no purpose, except to provide the opportunity to exercise a bit of twee suburban one-upmanship, and solve the dilemma about knitting pink or blue booties.

7. Water water everywhere!

Rule 1
This subject touches on incidents in the Bible, the only book at the top of the best-selling list which is never read. Some people take the facts in the Bible as literally true, that for example it was Moses coming down with the tablets that started us all taking pills.

Rule 2
Water, we are told, forms the largest percentage in the chemical make-up of the human body. Resist a growing tendency among inn-keepers to establish the same percentage in their whiskey.

Rule 3
A groom, about to go on his honeymoon cruise, bought a packet of condoms at his local chemists. As an afterthought, remembering his weakness at sea, he asked for a supply of Quells. The chemist frowned.

'If it makes you sick, why do you do it?' he asked.

Personal Case History
I was enjoying a Sunday morning lie-in, swapping fantasies between scoring the winning try for England at Twickenham, and being clutched to the warm bosom of an adoring Hollywood sex queen, when a piercing scream echoed from the area of the kitchen. I shot out of bed and scurried down the stairs, because the duchess quite sensibly reserves her scream for important occasions, and I imagined that she must have at least found a mutilated corpse in the deep-freeze, or our pet poodle swinging from the clothes drier with a suicide

note clenched between its teeth.

'Look at all this water!' she screeched. 'Don't just stand there! Help me!'

A thin film of water had leaked from the washing-machine and oozed on to the kitchen floor, and she already had thrown down a mopping-up blanket and was stamping up and down on it like a rabid grape-treader.

'This,' I said to myself, 'does not deserve a scream. Clearly my beloved has a phobia about water.' Nothing else could explain the frenzy of a wife who can pick up creepy-crawlies and snatch Daddy-long-legs in mid-air, repair electrical explosions with petulant *sang froid*, and watch the removal of polyps from the lower gut in glorious plasmacolour on t.v. medical programmes, without so much as a flinch.

But why did this come to me as a surprise, you may ask? I can only conclude that these primeval funks and irrational repugnancies from which we all suffer, sometimes become apparent quite late in married life.

It took a year for my daughter-in-law to discover my son had a fear of heights; he froze petrified on the second rung of the step-ladder when reaching up for a cake tin. We could have warned her, but we didn't know ourselves. The only previous clue I was given about the duchess's aquaphobia (if I may coin a word) was that she feels sea-sick standing on a wet plank, and would cheerfully swim the Channel rather than take the cross-Channel ferry. I began to notice after the kitchen incident that, although she remained fearless when it came to hearing bumps in the night and was the first to leap out of bed armed with a heavy vase; at the first sound of an unaccountable drip of water she turned into a wobbling jelly of fear and panic. By luck, our fears complement each other. I have no fear of water and would gladly dive into the stuff to save the kitchen from drowning, but my first and last impulse on hearing a bump in the night is to dive into the dirty-clothes basket.

I was prepared to leave the matter there; content only to warn newly-weds not to be alarmed by these sudden alien traits of character. Don't be dumb-struck or embarrassed if your wife drops her knitting and without warning shins up the standard lamp like a Gibbon monkey and points a quivering finger at the carpet, shrieking 'A spider! Kill it! Kill it quick!'. Only be embarrassed if, on climbing up the standard lamp, she finds you already up there. But there again, we can't pick and choose our phobias.

As it happened, however, my team of resident psychoanalysts (the regulars at the *Anchor and Hope*) brought up the subject of phobias a week later.

The thin gin and tonic (lemon and no ice) was telling the story of how her husband, a 16 stone best bitter, shut himself in the toilet until she had killed a moth. The discussion on phobias became general, and one sallow-complexioned campari and soda swore that if his wife had written all her phobias down (which included an allergy towards him) before they had married, he would have left her waiting at the altar.

Although personal phobias ranged between fire and bed bugs, water, once I had introduced the element, was almost universally feared by the females on the drinking panel. One amply built dry white wine shuddered.

'You'd never get me near a boat,' she whispered. 'I just go frantic at the thought of the sheer *depth* of water underneath.'

Sort that one out Mr. Freud.

'The interesting thing,' I said to the duchess afterwards, 'was that none of the women minded being *in* water - as per swimming - and none of them minded being under it - as per having a shower. What seemed to scare the daylights out of them was the thought of being *on* it. Now why is that?'

'I don't know,' she shivered. 'But I would hate to be Noah's wife, stuck in that Ark for forty days and nights.'

I struggled with the thought. Maybe phobias find their

origin in those primeval days, and if I could rationalise the duchess's fears to the point where she laughed gaily when pipes burst and water tanks overflowed, I would be out of the doghouse for being late back from the pub and ruining the lunch.

'I think you've got something there. The reason why most women shudder at the sight of snakes may go back to Eve, and how the serpent broke up the happy home in Paradise.'

'In that case,' she rejoined, 'women would also shudder at the sight of apples. But they don't.'

She had a point there too, although not such as a good one. After all, it was the serpent who seduced Eve into tasting the tree of knowledge, not the apple.

I turned to Genesis 7, 8, and 9 to see if there was anything in the Noah's Ark story to release my damsel from being in thrall and restore my position as her White Knight.

There was no evidence in the story that Mrs. Noah refused to go on board (the duchess certainly would have, until the weather report guaranteed forty days of calm seas). However, there was internal evidence that she might have walked up the gangway with fear and trepidation in her heart.

Take the length of the boat itself. God's specification was that it must be 300 cubits long. A cubit, if several dictionaries are to be believed, is the distance between the elbow and the tip of the middle finger, i.e. about an average of 20 inches. This would make the Ark about 170 yards long, which is 10 yards longer than the rugby pitch at the aforementioned Twickenham. Although Noah had three sons and three daughters-in-law and his wife to help him out, he must have been a pretty dab hand at D.I.Y. to knock up a boat that long, especially as God laid it down (He did a lot of that in the Old Testament) that there should be three decks; and more especially because Noah was 600 years old. He must have been a 1000 years old by the time he finished it. Then you have to take into account that the whole craft was made out of gopher wood and pitch, with two of everything on board from elephants down, plus the family furniture.

As this do-it-yourself effort, swaying like an over-loaded ferry boat, rose on the Flood, how Mrs. Noah must have agonised as to whether she had been right putting the world's zoo on the orlop deck, where a whole bunch of hippopotami, rhinoceroses, water buffalo and arctic bears could go crashing through the gopher wood and splitting a great hole in the hull: or whether the pitch would be a strong enough glue to hold the whole Heath Robinson device together. How she must have roamed the decks every night with candle held aloft in dread of finding a leak. How she must have fretted that her sons Ham, Shem, and Japheth, might not survive to be able to begat, so leaving great holes in Genesis 9 and 10. There were no carley rafts in those days and God forgot to lay anything down about lifeboats.

Oh yes! Some primitive gene in Mrs. Noah's body, the repository of her manic terrors of a watery grave, must have been begatted down the ages and thus account for the female obsession with untamed water.

'Deep down,' I summed up to the duchess after I had gone through the whole hypothesis, 'you are all afraid of a Second Flood, and of a hole in the bottom of your personal Ark.'

She drained her coffee, looked at me for a few seconds chewing ruminative lips and then rose from the table.

'Rubbish,' she said.

Helpful Hint

If you are scared of the sea, scared of flying, and a sufferer from car sickness, make the journey however long by bike. In terms of today's modern travel you will arrive sooner.

8. What every child knows about sex and the parents are afraid to ask

Rule 1
You will not discover your daughter's sexual *savoir-faire* and street cred directly. Wait until she is sipping a drink and say, 'This prostitute said to her customer "You've got a very small organ." And he said, "It's never played in a cathedral before."' If your daughter spits her drink out, you know you'd better keep an eye on her.

Rule 2
Do not think because your daughter is ugly - so ugly that even if she played Lady Godiva everyone would look at the horse - she will be devoid of sexual excess... It's mostly the ugly ones who believe in sex before marriage because nobody is going to marry them.

Rule 3
Keep a sense of proportion. As parents you will no doubt desire your son or daughter to grow up without developing grubby sexual habits, visiting sleazy strip-joints, indulging in casual sexual intercourse, but to be cleaning-living, decent human beings. But they can't be all *that* different to you.

Personal Case History
Young people know far more about sex than when I was their age. In fact they know far more about sex than I do at my present age. Some elders complain that when they were young, sex wasn't discussed. In my day it wasn't even known. Not being a girl I wasn't the recipient of the only piece of sex education passed on by mothers to their daughters about

the time they had a regular boy-friend. 'It's better if you wait.' Our neighbourhood was full of girls waiting; they didn't exactly know what *it* was because nobody told them. They took their mothers' advice on trust and didn't test the logic of the advice. If their mothers had all waited, how did they know it was better than not waiting? Presumably then, they *hadn't* waited, because only in that way could they have regretted their impetuosity and realised the superiority of putting their libidos on hold.

It was all very confusing. Especially to the ardent lover who had gone through all the approved stages of foreplay and was about to administer the coup-de-grace.

'It's better if we wait.'

'What now? How long for?'

Virginity in those days was something like a bus ticket - you hung on to it without quite knowing the reason why.

So where does this all leave us these days? In my concern to protect the institution of marriage, can I offer any advice about teaching children the *facts of life* which is of any value? That duty has long since been dumped into the lap of the schoolteacher. Schools are so proficient in sex education today that a regular bunch of girls are pregnant by the time they are thirteen. School outfitters are now producing a steady line in maternity drill slips. Yet educationalists continue to howl about the prevalence of sex ignorance - is it I who needs carting off to the funny farm or they?

A case could be made out that if a girl of thirteen produces an offspring, she isn't ignorant in sex, she has passed her 'A' levels. Couldn't a plea be made to distinguish between sexual ignorance and sexual innocence, because damn it all, if you sit a girl down on the front seat of a car and explain all the mechanics, it's only natural that she'll want to drive it?

Besides all that, do parents bother to find out exactly what is taught their offspring at these sex lessons? I'll wager they never ask.

Not so the duchess. Our youngest was the first to be taught the rudiments under the new era of enlightenment and she wasn't going to escape without a grilling.

'So what exactly did they teach you at this first lesson?'
'If you giggle you get thrown out.'

There is a lot to be said for a return to the old D.I.Y. method of the parents explaining the facts of life to their children - because they usually make such a mess of it, it puts the children off sex for a good five years. More important perhaps, they have a better idea when their young charges are of the right age to be enlightened.

The duchess: 'Isn't it about time you spoke to Paul?'
'I spoke to him this morning.'
'I don't mean that, I mean about the facts of life.'
'Why don't you speak to him?'
'I'll take on the daughters, you take on the sons.' (At that time we had no daughters)
'Oh.'
I'll admit here and now I am a yellow belt in cowardice when it comes to that sort of thing. After all, the sex act is

not a very lovely thing to describe. Leonardo da Vinci never painted it, Shakespeare never wrote a sonnet about it, Rodin stopped short at the kiss, and the only one to try and put it into poetic perspective was D.H. Lawrence whose book was banned for sixty years and labelled pornography - an ironic case where an author was hoisted on his own coinage.

Movie directors during the 80's thought it was *de rigueur* to include one scene of the act, but no matter how they portrayed it - in *slo-mo* with multiple soft mixes, and to the accompaniment of a Rachmaninoff slow movement, it all looked like humping in the end. Restless audiences couldn't wait for the scene next morning when the heroine, who had been naked all night, for some obscure reason clutched the duvet tightly round her in a pathetic display of bashfulness to prevent her lover from viewing her bosom. Never mind, it was the signal that the plot was being restarted. God in his wisdom has made the copulative act look embarrassingly ridiculous to the voyeur, and the first artist in words, clay, or paint who makes it look a thing of beauty deserves a Nobel Prize.

I wasn't exactly a Ph.D. on the subject myself. My sex education was normal. Playing mothers and fathers in the Rec. Comparing genitalia notes in puberty. Flirting with schoolgirls (inveterate in the hunt and impotent at the kill). And a post-graduate course in Dr. Marie Stopes, plus the standard lecture in the services on the perils of V.D. and G.P.I. (General Paralysis of the Insane - a beatific state one arrived at if one couldn't leave it alone).

'I know it isn't easy,' said the duchess smoothing out a crinkled sheet with a swish of the hot iron. 'But I don't want him brought up on what he learns from his mates at school.'

'I did.'

The duchess sniffed. 'And look where that got you,' she retorted enigmatically.

Over the next few days I agonised over the sort of

approach that would give a ten year-old the maximum enlightenment and me the minimum embarrassment.

'Right son, (opening the garage door) . . . You've already found out that boys have got - a thing and girls have got - a whatsit. Damnit no, I can't go on calling them a thing and a whatsit all night . . . (slipping into third gear and passing the morning milk-float) . . . Look - I'll tell you what - let's give all things make-up names. That's it! So let's say you and I have got a croinge, except that my croinge is a bit bigger than yours but forget that, that's not important . . . (Parking car at the station) . . . And the girl has got a lonk. Right? And when they get together to reproduce and the croinge goes into the lonk, that's called jigbuglio - er - jigbuglioing. (Buying morning paper and wandering onto station platform) . . . I think I've really got something going here, with luck I might get round mentioning the orgasm. (Sitting in crowded compartment) . . . Now, where was I? Ah yes. Now - you've probably noticed that on occasions without warning, your croinge goes as stiff as a poker . . .'

I am wondering why everybody in the compartment is staring at me. The hot horror of a blush burns my cheeks. Good heavens! Did I say that bit out loud? Could I have done? A rather insipid bank-clerk type is throwing me an inviting smile . . .

I staggered down to the psychiatric department that evening and asked my fellow inmates in the saloon bar of the *Anchor and Hope* for advice. I swigged a glass of *Auld Rob Roy* whisky, which the landlord claims is as good as whisky.

'I need help fellers,' I croaked. 'The duchess has given me a deadline. Has anybody told their kids the facts of life?'

'Charlie,' called by fellow bar-leaner, 'you're wanted.'

'What's Charlie done?' I asked.

'Told his kids.'

I allowed Charlie. His face was so pock-marked he looked like a scorer for a very bad darts team, but he was a regular.

'The trouble I'm having,' I explained to Charlie, after buying him the obligatory pint, 'is finding *les mots justes,* so to speak. The crunch time it seems to me is when he asks "But why do you do it?" and you get involved in all that rubbish about libido and orgasms. I mean what do you say to him? "Well you see son, you get this wonderful sensation, you see..."'

Charlie threw at me a dismissive gesture.

'Look, take my advice and just jump in with both feet. I gave them both barrels, no holes barred.'

'Them?'

'Two sons. The wife said it was a job lot. So I went straight into it. All the scientific terms - recrudescence and detumescence - all the slang words - all the dirty words. The lot. I didn't even leave room for questions.'

'What's recrudescence and detumescence?' I asked.

'How do I know? Anyway, that's my way, slap it on the block and let them sort out the final.'

'What happened? ' I asked hollow-eyed.

'Oh - they just looked at each other and one said, "Do you and mum do that?" And I said, "Of course." And they both looked at each other and said, "Urgh!" and walked out.'

Helpful Hint

Create the atmosphere of freedom of discussion among your growing family about the subject of sex, and mention terms like orgasmic retardation, premature ejaculation, recrudescence and detumescence without fear to stimulate curiosity. With luck they might explain things to you.

9. How To Stay Married Without Living Together

Rule 1
Marriage involves cohabitation, but cohabitation doesn't make a marriage.

Rule 2
'My dad can beat your dad!' boasted the Hollywood kid.
'Don't be daft,' said the other. 'Your dad *is* my dad!'
Hollywood, described as the place where one lies on the sand and gazes at the stars - and vice-versa - has its own rules. Marriage is what a gentleman enters into so that his previous bedfellow can claim for her services with alimony.

Rule 3
If you are unavoidably separated from your wife for long periods, either bear her gifts regularly on your return, or none at all. A surprise one-off gift is a dead giveaway that you are dipping your bucket in a far-off well.

Personal Case History
The duchess was watching *Come Dancing* whilst casting on a new piece of crochet work; I was on page 204 of the instructional manual of our new V.C.R. machine.
'Susan Plunk is a housewife,' cooed the t.v. announcer, as the couple on the screen jerked and twitched their way through what they call a tango these days. 'And her partner Harry Perkins is a lorry driver from Penge. They've been dancing together for ten years . . .'
The duchess let out a 'Ha!' of disbelief that could have

matched Queen Elizabeth's when Essex told her he had been kept late at the barracks.

'Housewife! How can she call herself a housewife when she's gallivanting all over the country with a lorry driver? I don't know how they get away with it, I really don't. What must her husband think? Surely he doesn't believe they're dancing together all the time?'

'I know some husbands,' I muttered, 'who would give their right arms to find a lorry driver to take their wives off their hands.'

'Housewife!' she snorted again, in the tone of one who wouldn't allow the Susan Plunks of this world to come within a hundred miles of that little band of women. 'She's the sort of mother whose kids end up on street corners sniffing glue. Did you read about that girl of thirteen who was raped and murdered in the woods this week? They said on the news that she went out at eleven o'clock and wasn't seen again. Now what sort of mother would allow a child of thirteen to go out at eleven o'clock at night and not even say where she is going?'

'It couldn't have been Susan Plunk,' I observed, 'because she was out dancing with her lorry driver.'

'Exactly. Women like her,' she prodded a crochet needle at the offensive Plunk executing a final galvanic spasm and panting in her partner's arms,' should never be allowed to get married. She's a good-time tart.'

'Are you suggesting,' I said in mock horror, 'that Mr. Perkins is having his wicked way with Mrs Plunk, unbeknownst to Mr. Plunk?'

'No. I'm suggesting it's knownst to Mr. Plunk. After ten years of it? If he doesn't knownst it now he never will. He probably encourages it, so he can be left alone to booze out of beer cans, while the kids are out on the street . . .'

'Sniffing glue. Yes, I get the picture,' I said, recognising that the duchess can swing almost any scene round to her favourite topic of neglectful parents. If she were on the BBC's adjudicating panel it wouldn't matter if the couple danced like Fred Astaire and Ginger Rogers, if they couldn't prove they were man and wife and the kids were off hand, she would give them zilch points. Still it set me thinking about the Susan Plunks and Harry Perkins of this world.

Superficially the married world is divided into those who still live in a state of holy matrimony and those who have divorced in a state of unholy acrimony, but in fact a vast number of couples occupy that no man's land in between, who remain married, but from whom the thrill of togetherness has long since departed. Neither love nor hate pervades in their homes, only the inertial habit of sharing the same premises as a lesser evil to the upheaval of divorce. Staying married without actually living together (in the full sense implied in the words of the wedding ceremony) is the compromise settled for under many a roof in Britain.

(It is perhaps an irony that many a couple who are branded as *living together* in the pejorative sense - it used to be called *living in sin* - make a better job of it than those couples who have promised to do so in church.)

Dear brides of the future, better include in your trousseau a few precepts of wisdom, rather than a hair dryer and a spare dress. Infidelity on the part of your husband is less likely in the sexual sense than infidelity to the whole concept of sharing your lives together. And ah yes! I'm ashamed to confess it, but the male gender is, despite the odd Susan Plunk, the principal backslider.

Do not look for an illicit love affair, look for that more elusive sin - frequent non-presence in the home. The husband is partially married to the macho sub-culture of *getting away from the wife and kids* on any excuse. In fact, so popular is the practice, wars, revolutions, and the historic founding of nations could be attributed to man's attempt to be anything else but a domesticated animal.

Take the Crusades. History describes them as a holy war by the Christians against the threat of Islam. But they went on for 200 years, and I've never known the British to be enthusiastic about anything for 200 years except for booze and football, so there must have been some other attraction. The attraction to any crusader was the two years away from cutting the grass, doing the washing up, and getting the kids off the wife's hands by taking them to the park. Add to that a trip through the flesh pots of Europe, a bash or two at the foreigners, and a build-up of the duty-frees before coming home and unlocking the wife's chastity belt. No wonder the Crusades were run by kings to create a sense of national unity. ('Put me down for the next one guv!') How could you get nagged for coming home a hero loaded with silks, spices, body oils, and sugared almonds?

In truth, wars, for those who don't get shot or blown up in them, are a favoured alternative to marital bondage. Mention World War II to a service veteran and a nostalgic gleam comes into his eyes. What better life can be imagined than that of being free all the year round from domestic responsibility except for that of humping the wife when on leave?

We can assume, in our unique interpretation of history, that wives cottoned on to this dodge over the centuries and have gradually set a time limit to wars as being too much of a good thing. The 200 year-long Crusades were followed by the Hundred Years War, which was followed by the Thirty Years War, the Seven Years War, the Great War (4 years), and World War II (5 years), the Falklands War (months), and the Gulf War (days). Jewish mothers (who want to know where their husbands are if they take ten seconds longer taking out the trash) achieved the record with a Six Day War. If it had taken any longer they would have told their husbands to surrender and come back home.

The nuclear bomb can be viewed not as the result of man's attempt to discover ever greater means of mass destruction, but as an outcome of housewifely pressure to find a way of getting a war over with in minutes.

In the craft of excusable absenteeism from the home, crusades and wars are still going on, only in peace time they are called Test Match Tours abroad. The same heroic medals are up for grabs in the event of victory but, more to the point, a cricketer of Test Match standard can rely on the early and middle years of his married life being spent away from domestic obligations for a goodly portion of each year - longer if he becomes a coach or a tour manager. His only problem is to sound sincere when he complains about being separated from his family.

On the same basis, dear bride, if you are not a Susan Plunk, and your modest dream is that of cosy domestic bliss in a mock-Tudor in Oxted, do not marry a tour golfer, a pro tennis player, an amateur athlete with Olympic ambitions, any rugby player with or without ambitions, a motor-racing driver or mechanic, or indeed anyone belonging to the sporting fraternity, because they have all copied the cricketers' example, globe-trotting in search of enemies to fight and overcome, for the money or for the glory, and mainly for the long periods of respite from the drudgeries of domestic life.

This absentee list should also include merchant seamen, airline pilots and personnel, overseas sales representatives, foreign service diplomats, movie directors and technicians, archeologists, oceanographers, oil-rig workers, wine-tasters, and package tour couriers, none of whom can earn enough to pay for the weekly newspapers without going 2000 miles or spending six months away from home; and who, one suspects, were attracted to those occupations in the first instance because they provided an unassailable leave of absence from home if by a stroke of bad luck they fell in love and married.

The next time you watch *This Natural World* and are told that it took two years to film the life-cycle of the lesser-crested bird of paradise, think of the cameraman spending all his weekends living it up in some Peruvian country club, (paid for by you via your t.v. licence), and think of his poor wife at home waiting for the bloody bird of paradise to copulate and get it all over and done with.

But there are other escape routes from the tiresome drag of having to live together with your wife if you are not inclined to be a globe-trotter. The rich provided their own solution. When they promised to 'live together in a state of holy matrimony' they made sure it was a damned big estate, providing them with enough bolt-holes to keep them away from the family. Take Buckingham Palace. If Prince Philip found the Queen in a scratchy mood, he could, with a bit of dodging about and the help of a couple of venal butlers, avoid bumping into her for days on end. (As Proverbs lets it drop in xxi. 9. *It is better to dwell in the corner of the housetop than with a brawling woman in a wide House*). He could always tell the butler to say he was in the library, and by the time the Queen had got to the library, he could have dodged up the back stairs to the Green Room, and by the time she got there, he could have nipped out to the front yard to have a chat to the sentries, or out on to the balcony to give the tourists a couple of free waves.

Why else would they build those enormous castles, stately homes, and sprawling pile of bricks like Blenheim Palace? It couldn't have been because they expected a large family. Not even an Italian-Pakistani kibbutz with libidos on after-burn could fill 250 bedrooms.

But wealth, girls, is not a *sin qua non* for male domestic escapism. Watch out for the quiet suburban type mouse who nevertheless gradually builds up his bolt-holes Lego block fashion, over the years: the shed at the bottom of the garden, the workshop in the garage, the atelier in the attic, and the local allotment just by *The Fox and Hounds*. Above all beware of the society and club enthusiast, for his withdrawal from the pact of togetherness is imperceptibly languid: he doesn't stride away, he minces on tiptoe. As an example, take Toby Davies, almost a friend of ours. He started his married life as a weekend cricketer. Then he joined the tennis club, the local trout fishing club, and then the Freemasons. He is now the treasurer of three lodges, the Chairman of the Cricket Club, the auditor of a rugby club, on the committee of the trout fishing club and bee-keeping society, and secretary of a livery company's golfing society. This takes care of most weekends in the year, most nights a week, and odd swan-offs on outings and Easter Tours, and we have to book weeks ahead to invite him and his wife round to dinner - if we ever felt inclined to. ('It's only to give her a night out poor soul.')

What is with these fellows? Surely they should have not bothered about getting married at all and have settled for a paid housekeeper with easy morals?

Ah well, now the ladies have caught on to the racket; which brings us back to Susan Plunk. There she twirls, with her lacquered coiffure, her glow lipstick smile, and her flashing legs, self-sealed inside a world of substitute glamour. And why not? Because hasn't she been urged in a thousand Women's Lib clichés to 'do her own thing', 'find out who she really is and where she is at'?

Despite the duchess's calumny, Susan Plunk is only doing what men have done for centuries living in a condition of undivorce.

Perhaps God could put reproduction *on hold* whilst the two sexes sort out what they really want. Meanwhile the duchess has crocheted ten more rows, and I am fetching our ten year-old to tell me how to work the V.C.R. machine.

Helpful Hint

Marriage is rather like a car: it needs constant servicing and maintenance to keep it running from the very first day. If, for example, you as a bride have indulged in pre-marital sex with your husband, it is a good tip on your honeymoon night to wear a flimsy see-through nightdress wearing wellies and a bucket over your head . . . after all you've got to surprise him with something.

10. Don't die on a Friday

Rule 1
If one believed everything that was engraved on tombstones, one could only assume that all the bastards must have been cremated.

Rule 2
The vicar invited anyone from the small group gathered round the grave to say a few kind words about the departed. His invitation was greeted with a long stony silence until a voice was heard at the back.

'Well I'll say this for him - his brother was worse.'

To avoid embarrassment at your own funeral, send a bottle of Scotch now and again to a friend as soon as you start to feel your wheels dropping off.

Rule 3
It is quite wrong to compare marriage with 'a life sentence': in the latter you gain remission for good behaviour.

Personal Case History
A literary-minded pink gin in the Psychiatric ward of the *Anchor and Hope* pointed out that Man is fundamentally an optimist. He quoted *The Oxford Book of Quotations*:

'There are five and a half columns in the index involving the word *life*, and only three and a half columns of quotations involving the word *death*,' he observed.

'Well stop trying to redress the balance,' sniffed his wife, eyeing his third pink gin.

A morose pint of Guinness said that may be the case, but the older he became, the more rapidly his old friends were joining the three and a half columns.

'Once you're past 65,' he muttered sadly, 'you find yourself attending more funerals than weddings.'

The subject of the Grim Reaper invariably arises at the *Anchor and Hope*. Morbidity sets in after the fourth or fifth round of drinks, and especially prone are the inmates within walking distance of the pub who can enjoy a fourth or fifth round, at least until the law changes and one can be arrested for being drunk in charge of an umbrella.

'Look on the bright side old man,' said the pink gin, slapping the Guinness on the back. 'And remember the words of Sir Thomas Browne - *Death is a cure of all diseases*'

'When it comes to my arthritis, I'll stick to aspirin if you don't mind,' rejoined his companion. 'Chucking myself off a cliff strikes me as a bit of a drastic way of getting rid of painful joints.'

'Good heavens I wasn't suggesting suicide,' said the other. 'No good old man. The insurance people won't pay up and everybody starts contesting your will. No no. Just get someone to shoot you!' He laughed uproariously.

'If he stays here any longer,' I observed, glancing at the clock, 'his wife is going to do that anyway.' I could afford to be smug, the duchess was with me.

The subject of making a will having been touched on, the duchess on the way home suggested we did the same.

'Isn't it a bit early for that?' I asked defensively. 'I mean circumstances change and you have to keep making out new ones.'

'So you make out a new one,' she said. 'But what happens if you get run down by a bus tomorrow?'

'It seems to me,' I complained, 'that ever since we got married, you've had this long line of hypothetical buses queuing up, waiting to knock me down when you give the signal. Whenever the subject of insurance, money, or wills crops up, there's a bus lurking round the corner.'

I knew I was protesting in vain. Once the duchess had mentally scribbled a note on her brain's memo pad, it was never erased until it had been dealt with.

Accordingly, over the next few weeks we sat glassy-eyed on the other side of a solicitor's table while he steered us through the complexities of executors, trusts, and probates.

'There is one thing I am going to do,' I said to my immediate executrix (if I popped off first). 'I'm going to leave my body to medical science. After all, it might be useful in these days of transplants and what have you. And it will save that ridiculous cost they charge for funerals.'

The duchess gave me a pitiful look.

'I don't know what use they will make of your body,' she exclaimed. 'Your liver and lungs must be in a terrible state after all that drinking and smoking. After forty years of rugby your hips are out of line, your nose is broken, your toe nails keep falling out and you've got athlete's foot.'

I shrugged.

'They'll chuck out what they don't want. But my penis is in good shape.'

The duchess threw me a look which couldn't make up its mind whether to be in scorn or gratitude.

'It's going to be no use to anyone if you don't die until you're ninety.'

'On the contrary, it will be very useful to a randy old man of ninety-two.'

Crossing over the footbridge of our neighbouring stream, she came to a decision.

'Well if you're going to do it, I shall do it.'

'You haven't got one.'

She punched me.

'You know what I mean. My body is in a darn sight better condition than yours.'

I nodded.

'Except for the battle scars of motherhood, you are

virtually Venus de Milo. You still have a sylph-like figure - if you can imagine a slightly fuller sylph.'

'And I love you too,' she murmured, giving me a peck with an admonishing squeeze in the scrotum area.

I wonder if the Queen does that sort of thing to Phil?

'I'm virtually Venus de Milo'

A week or so later we were driving along in the car and the duchess said,

'Oh by the way! I was talking to Doris about leaving our bodies to medical science and she said that she was going to do that too. But she said, "Don't die on a Friday."'

'Don't die on a Friday? I thought Jesus died on a Friday. You know - Good Friday?'

'Maybe he did, but he didn't leave his body to medical science did he? Anyway Doris said Roy left his body to medical science,' (Roy was Doris's departed husband) 'and when the body arrived at the hospital, the pathological department, or whatever it was, just said that everybody goes home on a Friday, and they just left it there until Monday. Can you believe that? So it was all wasted. They scream out for hearts and eyes and things and just left his body there until it was too late.'

Citizens of lengthening years take note: if you suspect that your dying throb is coming on during a Friday, try to stick it out until Monday; the couple of good ounces left in your corpse will have a better chance of being put to use.

One final obstacle has to be overcome, mollifying the sensibilities of your family. They may not like the idea of dumping your cadaver on the butcher's block even if you do. Our eldest when told of our decision swayed slightly.

'Don't worry, you can hold a memorial service immediately,' comforted the duchess. 'In fact a lot of hospitals arrange it for you.'

'After all, a memorial service is just a funeral without the coffin,' I added cheerfully.

He seemed pacified. I nursed in my bosom the hope that in introducing this macabre subject, our offspring would at least accord us respect for facing up to the unpalatable subject of our own deaths and coming to a decision. Too often it is thrust into the background, and even more often the burden is thrown upon one unfortunate family member to deal with.

As an aftermath to this event, the duchess, crocheting reflectively muttered,

'I know that a penis can be transplanted, but can it ever get an erection?'

'It couldn't help it if it saw a figure like yours dear,' I replied.

As an old fly-half I had never lost my eye for half an opening.

Helpful Hint

If we really believed in reincarnation we would leave all our money to ourselves.

11. On the advantages of being nagged

Rule 1
Remember fellers, the only reason why a man can say what he likes in his own home is because nobody listens to him.

Rule 2
They say wives grow up to be like their mothers. But don't look at her mother, look at her father. That's you in 20 years!

Rule 3
If you have a nagging wife, install some goldfish in the house ... Watching mouths open and close all day without a sound coming out has a therapeutic value.

Personal Case History
'I'm not nagging you,' the duchess is wont to say gently. 'I'm just telling you.' But I never could tell the difference.

Nagging has been going on since - well since before the days when Felix Aylmer had hair. As a cause for breaking up marriages I think it has been overstressed. Roger Boswell and Ray Allcock, two well-known victims of notorious naggers on our particular patch, have been nagged skinny for years, but apart from the violent twitches they behave quite normally. Maybe they are born masochists who like to be verbally flagellated, or have simply become inured to it in much the same way a Mancunian hardly notices the rain, an Eskimo the cold, or an Aussie the cloud of flies buzzing round his head like a live busby.

Admittedly, even from the gentlest of wives, nagging does have a mild hypnotic effect on the naggee because of its unremitting nature. ('Please don't leave the hot water tap trickling, it wastes fuel . . . Don't drive so fast . . . Do you need that cigarette? . . . I've mentioned three times that the lawn needs cutting . . . When are you going to show an interest in your child's education? . . . That's the third whiskey you've had . . . You should stick up for yourself for once . . . You left the bowl smeared with toothpaste again . . .'

Why is it that so many wives devote their lives to the expurgation of their husbands' imperfections and to the remoulding of them into the shape of their own images? So universal is the pursuit one begins to suspect that nagging, and all that goes with it, is hereditary - a code in the female DNA helix passed on from one generation to another.

I'm inclined to support that theory and trace it all back to Eve. The guilt of causing her hubby's being thrown out of Paradise by eating the apple must have weighed heavily upon her. You can imagine how she felt, hardly assuaged by now having to wear a fig leaf in an intimate place. Adam would have to fight hard to earn a *Club Class* ticket back to Heaven. In recompense, she devoted her life to making him as perfect as possible.

> *For nothing lovelier can be found*
> *In woman, than to study household good,*
> *And good works in her husband to promote.*

Well there you are, John Milton backs me up, to which he should have added:

> *E'en though her lifetime task behoveth*
> *Her, to nag the lazy lump to death.*

Since then, in my view, every daughter of Eve has been infected by the same bug, and can't wait, metaphorically speaking, to throw the shapeless bulk of her husband onto the sculptor's block and start chipping and chiselling. It doesn't say much for what she thought of him to marry him, but they say love is blind, and what woman has ever let love get in the way of anything she really wants? In the end, as the pretty girl said, a woman is a sex all unto herself.

Accepting the hypothesis that nagging is only indulged in for the husband's spiritual welfare, it is perhaps the only advantage to be got out of it, and I would urge new husbands under attack to clutch on to this straw. At least it proves that the wife thinks the husband is still redeemable and worthy of attention. And maybe he would prefer his wife to nag him, than for her to go to bingo five nights a week, or to take to gin and keep falling over in the High Street.

As to myself, after many years of corrective training by the duchess, I am still many beatitudes away from sainthood, but I appreciate what she is trying to do, and if I fail the entrance exam at the Pearly Gates it won't be because she hasn't done her best. Indifference, after all, is the woodworm of marriage, and I certainly can't complain that our relationship is suffering from that.

I wish I could offer something more concrete but unfortunately nagging isn't rated as social crime along with wife-beating or child neglect warranting a Royal Society or a National Institution to prevent it.

It's not even considered evidence at the Old Bailey when a poor victim claims that it was his wife's nagging which caused him to bury a hatchet in her head. We can see the prosecuting counsel smirking.

'M'Lud - if we all buried hatchets into our wives' heads just because they were nagging us, there would very soon be a dearth of hatchets!'

The Judge notes on his pad, *Buy hatchet tomorrow*.

A case could be made out for instituting a *Victims' Support Group* or a *Naggers Anonymous*, but I doubt if group therapy would work with naggees. A man doesn't lack the courage to stand up among his peers and confess 'I am an alcoholic', but he draws the line at breaking into tears and blubbering 'I am a henpecked husband!'

Far better, the next time he hears 'Where the hell have you been?' or 'Can I ask you not to walk in from the garden with your muddy shoes' or 'You haven't wasted money on buying another golf putter have you?', that he looks fondly upon such comments as an altruistic desire by his partner to see his ashes safely on the way to Heaven before she collects the insurance. Sorry to be so wimpish on this subject, but you know how it is indoors fellers, it will be a miracle if even these notes ever appear . . .

Helpful Hint

The macho method. The first time your newly-wed starts nagging you, say nothing. Just show her a yellow card.

12. Spare the rod and spoil your retirement

Rule 1
Anticipate when your young one learns the first swear word. It could happen when you are entertaining the vicar to tea, and your well-brought-up kid enters on a pogo stick muttering in rhythm 'Bugger-bugger-bugger-bugger...'

Learn to deal with it calmly (a) by knocking the little bugger's head off, (b) by peeing into the tea-pot and creating a diversion.

Rule 2
Don't allow your child's behaviour to degenerate so much that when he goes to school you have to send him with a note to explain why he is there.

Rule 3
The choice in education for children is now enormous. You can either send him or her to a Comprehensive to study social politics, welfare and community work, and become an arrogant left-wing twit; or to a public school to become an athletic intellectual wizard somewhere to the far right of Atilla the Hun. The only advantage in the latter is that he can be trained to be an atomic scientist who can do the 100 metres in 10 seconds, and so be the farthest away when there's a radiation leak.

Personal Case History
The kids round our way today are not much different from us when we were kids round somebody else's way. They only seem different because hooliganism is given more prominence in the media these days; but then again

everything is given more prominence in the media these days, and I sometimes wonder if the world wouldn't be a better place if newspapers were cut down to two pages and television news to fifteen minutes. Nevertheless we are told that our youth is subject to waves of social and moral turpitude and all sorts of influences are ascribed to the cause. Just lately, there has been a focus on bullying at school with one school setting up a children's court to punish the offenders.

'Stupid people!' dismissed the duchess over morning coffee. 'It's the parents they should haul up before the school, not the kids.'

'Yes dear,' I said. I knew what was coming. She had a theory that pretty well every canker in society was caused by selfish, uncaring, and ignorant parents, and later added a codicil that parental responsibility decayed further with the invention of the disposable nappie.

'I don't quite see that,' I said at the time.

'You wouldn't,' she rejoined, 'because you didn't have to wash nappies. But when you had to wash clean and iron forty dirty nappies every week for a year and a half, you saw children in a different light.'

'What sort of light?' I asked interested.

'You still love them,' she said, 'but after cleaning up their muck for such a long time, you make darn sure they behave themselves, if only to make it all worthwhile.'

The case continues...

My only thought was that there were some young hooligans along our road whose parents should have kept the disposable nappies and thrown away the kids.

It is impossible to lay down rules about child discipline because it undergoes so many changes in fashion and emphasis. In the days of my youth the birch was in the courts, the cane was in the schools, and the leather strap was in the home. Even before the stings had faded on my palms (for sucking sweets, or talking, or flicking ink-pellets in class), they shifted the goalposts and flagellation was dismissed as barbaric: a last minute *volte face* to which I took strong objection: you can't ask for your punishments back, can you?

Home discipline fell back on the lesser sentence 'Go to your room! And don't come down until I tell you!' Those were the days when central-heating was confined to offices, schools, and cinemas, and the average child's bedroom was an ice box with a bed, a chair, and a chest of drawers, slightly less inviting than the average prison cell. Nowadays a *young person's* bedroom is a centrally-heated shrine to his or her pop idols, with posters depicting them screaming defiance into hand-mikes adorning the walls, and everywhere else are strewn the successive icons of each passing fad - teddy bears, Sindy and Snoopy dolls, skateboards, Scalextric, video war games, Sony Walkman, guitars, hi-fis, computers and colour t.v. sets. An equivalent punishment today would be 'Come out of your room! And don't go back in until I tell you!' Perhaps the thought of having to spend the whole evening with boring old mum and dad in the lounge would be daunting enough.

But what do we want of our children? Oscar Wilde's apothegm *children begin by loving their parents and by the time they have grown up sometimes forgive them* was intended as a joke to be challenged. Forgiveness seems a very poor reward, if indeed we deserve one. Young couples today who wish to stay married, worried about their wall-to-wall mortgage, cannot see far ahead to those retirement years when they will cherish the love and concern of their grown up brood; yet the down-payments towards that welcome recompense begin early, in fact as soon as the first-born sweeps his big baby eyes over the faces of his coochy-cooing parents and rewards them with a condescending grin. (How soon they start to calculate!)

So to whom do we turn for help and guidance? Surely not to 'Nurse Drew' in the Sunday newspaper, whose column is often written by the office boy. What about the Rock of Ages, the *Good Book*, and the word of the Lord? Now there's a thing. He brought up thousands of children - the children of Israel. He elected them his chosen people and when you scour through the pages of the Old Testament, you get the impression that he wished he'd chosen somebody else. A right bunch of contrary kids they turned out to be. They boast today that they were the first tribe to believe in only one God, but they failed to mention that God took about 2000 years to convince them that he was the one, 'I am the Lord thy God,' he thundered, 'and thou shalt worship me and only me.' 'O.K. boss,' they said. And the next minute they ran into a tribe that believed the moon was made of cream cheese and took up worshipping the moon.

It reminded me irresistibly of the duchess wagging her finger at our ten year-old.

'I don't care what Cynthia Wiggins' mother says, or what Daphne Diamond's mother says, I am your mother and you wear what I say!'

On the positive side the Lord was first-rate in keeping an open dialogue with his children. It needs only a riffle through Leviticus, Numbers, and Deuteronomy, to discover that he was no William Randolph Hearst, who opened his office door once a year and bellowed patriarchal pronouncements. On the contrary he was the doyen of feed-back, popping up from behind bushes and sand dunes, and asking what was going on, and who was doing what, and telling them what they were doing right and what they were doing wrong. A past master at combining praise and censure in one breath, when he wasn't blessing his brood and promising them all the riches of the Earth, he was waxing exceeding wrath at sinners and idolaters.

Once again I'm reminded of the duchess in full flood.

'Hallo dear! (kiss) How are you? What good news about your job! Aren't you pleased? I'm so glad for you. You're not drinking too much are you? And you really ought to do something about your hair. I'm so pleased to see you. Tell me all about it. You're looking terrible. Are you sleeping properly? ... etc'

I would be straining your credulity to stretch this analogy any further although there are some other whimsical parallels. When God was too busy he sent along one of his delegates like Moses. When the duchess is too busy she leaves me to pass on her messages.

I know I'm nothing like Moses, but in essence there isn't a lot of difference between his telling the children of Israel 'Thou shalt keep the Lord's commandments, and the statutes, and the judgements . . .' and my telling my brood, 'Now listen kids, your mother says you've got to do what you're told and behave yourselves'.

And I know that the duchess is nothing like God, and neither of us is even Jewish, but God did have a tough time raising his tribe and there's much to be learned from his efforts. Raising kids, we learn, is a bit like running a car: it's not the delivery that matters, it's the back-up service, and boy! did the children of Israel have a back-up service! Toyota's is not a patch on God's. Several thousand years and eight hundred pages later, he is still at it in Zechariah, grabbing the children of Israel by their ears, slapping their knees, and telling them not be horrible little swines like their dads and to listen to him.

'I've told you a million times,' the duchess would scold, 'not to go out in the evenings without telling me where you are going first!'

Oh yes, there is a close affinity here. Occasional doses of famine and pestilence are effective now again, but it is the daily spoonful of discipline and care and concern over the years which produces the best results.

Dear newlyweds, never give up showering your children with a mixture of warm love and cold reproof, and surely goodness and mercy shall follow all the days of the little blighters' lives. And if at your age of seventy the phone rings and your son or daughter say, 'Hallo Dad, how's everything at home?', you don't have to be told how well you have brought up your children.

Helpful Hint

According to the *Guinness Book of Records*, a Brazilian mother produced 24 sons and 8 daughters.

'I don't know what all the fuss is about,' said the father in a brief moment when he was caught in an upright position. His wife became an expert on ceilings. The hint is, don't go in for large families unless you can do whatever you do for a living very fast.

13. An eye for the birds

Rule 1
One of the world's most unkept promises: the son or daughter who begs to have a pet dog and swears to take it out for its daily walk.

Rule 2
A look at nature now and then restores our sense of proportion about sex. Nobody has yet tracked down a lesbian hippo or a gay giraffe, and few female warthogs say, 'You only want me for my body.'

Rule 3
It might be wise before marriage to consult your intended's views about caged animals . . . !

Personal Case History
Usually I am one of nature's bird lovers. Until the spring that is, when my cherry tree starts to fruit. Then I could cheerfully shoot the entire bird population that shares my estate. (One lawn, five apple trees, two plum, and one cherry).

The cherry happens to produce a sweet succulent White Heart. So the birds tell me, I've never tasted one. Every year the tree is laden, but not one orb of fruit has ever graced my fruit-bowl. For ten years I accepted the fate of the cherry-bereft. And then suddenly I thought to myself 'Why should they get away with it? Here am I, *homo sapiens*, endowed with superior cunning, not to mention the back-up of modern technology; surely I can scare away a few birds once a year?'

It was a foolhardy thought as it turned out, which nearly pushed me into insanity. The scientist who said the world would eventually be taken over by the insects and the birds was absolutely right.

What galled me most was the fact that not only did the birds eat every single cherry, they spat the pips out on the lawn. I went into deep research on the subject of bird scaring.

I opened up the first year of the war with the tried-and-true method of strips of rustling paper. Somebody also suggested microfoil, which sounded a good idea until I tried it. Have you ever tried to tie strips of microfoil on to branch stems waving capriciously in the breeze? The whole method failed because I couldn't successfully tie anything beyond reach without elaborate manoeuvres with the ladder, which took hours. Consequently the birds left me the bottom three feet of cherries (the green ones), and gobbled up the top forty-seven feet of the ripe ones.

'A red flag on the top,' opined the duchess in the second year of the war. 'I read it in a magazine somewhere. It's supposed to work.'

I don't know what the neighbours thought when they saw this idiot hoisting a red flag up his cherry-tree. I know what the birds thought: they thought I was putting up a signpost in case they forgot where the tree was. That year twice as many birds devoured the cherries in half the time, and somebody sprayed *Commie* on my garage doors.

By now the bird-scaring challenge had become an obsession. Every year I walked down the lawn with a new device, my two eldest sons collapsed with laughter.

The third year I saw on television a highly successful noise device. I couldn't afford miles of armoured cable and the sophisticated electronics, so I made my own version. This consisted of a tape recorder on which I had recorded spasmodic explosions, screams, and various Banshee noises. As I strode confidently down to the cherry tree armed with the tape recorder, the devouring flocks fluttered to nearby trees to watch. It was frightening in a kind of way, like a scene from Hitchcock's *The Birds*. One could almost hear them thinking, 'I wonder what the silly old fool is coming up with this year?'

I switched the tape-recorder on and retired to the patio deck-chair with a smirk on my face. The starlings and the finches fluttered back in twos and threes to their feeding ground. Then an almighty bang echoed round the garden. There was a yelp from over the fence and the old lady next door poked her head over and shouted,

'What the hell was that?'

I told her.

'I nearly put the fork through my foot,' she intoned threateningly. During the ensuing conversation I noticed that the birds hadn't budged an inch from their cherry-gobbling perches, and after about an hour the battery on the tape-recorder ran out.

Last year found me winding spools of old videotape round the tree's branches because somebody told me that it glistens in the sun and scares off the birds. It would have scared more birds away if I had put a television set in the tree and showed them a few hours of daytime television. As autumn turned to winter, the elements ravaged the videotape and the tree looked like a shell-blasted victim at Ypres, or the backdrop to the witches' scene in *Macbeth*. It took months to strip the darn stuff off and I was still digging up bits of it with my early spring potatoes.

If you know a good tip about bird scaring, stop me any time in the street and tell me, and I will punch you on the nose. You can't miss me around cherry time. I'm the one with a leery twitch and look a bit like Herbert Lom after an encounter with Inspector Clouseau.

Helpful Hint
On this subject it is better to keep one's advice to oneself.

14. What's in a name?

Rule 1
You will have observed that it is now a modern practice for employees in shops and supermarkets to have their Christian names prominently displayed on their chests. Do not be misled into thinking that by this device the proprietors have sportingly made their employees easily identifiable in cases of complaint. They are hoping that since you are now on first name terms with their Christines, and Normans and Vanessas, you'll hesitate before getting them into trouble.

Rule 2
Name your children wisely. If you don't believe in the power and efficacy of a name, replace 'My name is Bond - James Bond' with 'My name is Sludge - Fred Sludge.'

Rule 3
Nick-names are normally affectionate, except for those who actually earn names in the nick. (*Light-fingered Larry*, *Harry the Snitch*, *Razor-blade Ron*). Avoiding a pejorative nick-name depends on you.

'I call my mother-in-law *Exocet*: you can see her coming but you can't do a damn thing about it.'

'We called her *Door-Knob* because more hands had been laid on her than on one.'

Personal Case History
To misquote the Bard, a rose by any other name would smell as sweet, although it's hardly likely the rose will be given another name, it being so appropriate to the flower's delicacy and fragrance. Mankind is pretty good at naming things: a

warthog looks a warthog and a cowslip looks a cowslip; but we're not so hot at naming children because we have to do it so early, before the recipient has become, as it were, an identifiable object. Given the choice, parents would no doubt prefer the vicar to say 'I name this child Blank, pending future developments.' The duchess and I agonised for days over what to call our firstborn: by the time he was five we knew exactly what to call him.

Mention of the rose reminds me that when I was at infants' school, the names of flowers were in vogue for girls. I can make a safe bet at the *Anchor and Hope* that any woman named Marigold, Poppy, Lilly, Daisy, Rose, or Dahlia, is about the same age as myself. Names are a fairly accurate way of assessing age. Pramloads of Shirleys were poured into the streets following the messianic impact of Shirley Temple on the silver screen in the 'thirties, and the last of the Victorias and Alberts left us long ago.

In truth parents name their children out of an arbitrary mixture of pride, prejudice, inertia, hope, fashion, and sentiment. Of late a new motivation has become apparent. Whereas yesterday my playmates in school were called Charlie, Dave, Fred, Doris, or Elsie; today the names shrieked across playgrounds are Jason, Dirk, Tarquin, Abigail, Claire, and Josie. Names have now become a special weapon. Give a dog a good name, seems to run the theory, and it has a better chance at Crufts.

For example young parents in the struggling classes today nurse aspirations for their daughters of their eschewing the mundane jobs of yesteryear (as shop assistants, kiosk girls, waitresses, and office menials) and ascending into that decorative infrastructure formally occupied by debutantes, e.g. models, entertainment secretaries, public relations assistants, executives' hostesses, fashion promoters, and entrepreneurs.

For some reason such parents concluded that all

debutantes' names ended in an *a*, so that we are now knee-deep in young girls called Joella, Samantha, Isabella, Clovissa, Amanda, Tessa, Sandra, Belinda, Julia, Maria, Adriana, Anna, Sara, Priscilla, Miranda, Clarissa, Diana, Celia, and Tina, all walking about with clothes and hair-dos that have emptied their mothers' purses, heavy regional accents, one GCSE qualification, and high hopes.

'I know who you mean,' nodded our solicitor double-scotch at the bar. *Blind Date* hires them by the lorry-load.'

'I avoid all those Prunellas and Cassandras like the plague,' chipped in our local betting shop manager, buying the next round with his winnings from the 1.30. 'I prefer a Lil who spills crumbs down her and farts, provided she can add and subtract.'

'Is that a condition? That she farts?' queried the solicitor.

'You know what I mean. I had one of those Prunella girls once, and she handed me the calculator and said, "Can yew do this guv? I don't wanna damidge me nay-ools!" Damage her nay-ools! I admit she looked a million dollars when she first turned up, with short leather pants, legs up to her arse. But young girls today think that all they need do is walk around looking sexy. Then they complain if someone touches them up.'

'We knew why you fired her,' smiled the solicitor. 'Now we know why you hired her in the first place.'

'Sid hires them,' muttered a knowledgeable punter,' and his old woman fires them.'

I was set off on quite a different tack when the duchess tapped the bump of her first pregnancy and said,

'I don't mind what he or she is called, as long as it can't be shortened. There's nothing wrong with a Percy or a Margaret as long as it doesn't become *Perce* and *Maggie*. I hate that. Take your name. Richard is a nice name, but you became *Dick*.'

'Ah that was because my father was called Dick,' I explained. 'So when I was born I was called *Little Dick*: which was organically correct if nothing else.'

Thereafter I wasted a lot of time trying to think of a name that refused to be shortened. The acid test was whether the name resisted truncation as yelled across the school playground. Leslie inevitably became *Les*, Dennis became *Den*, Elizabeth became *Liz*, Ignatius became *Iggy*, and failing all other diminutives a Marmaduke became *Four Eyes* or *Swotter*.

So what's in a name? A lot more than we are disposed to think, perhaps. It's the one attribute in life bestowed upon us over which we have no control. First-time mothers please bear in mind, your children will be given names that they are stuck with for the rest of their lives. That little pink bundle that you so fondly see as a Melanie, growing up to be the fashion editor of *Vogue* may turn out to be a Fag Ash Lil with the brains of a bucket.

Semantic overtones cling to names like glue and it takes a strong personality to shake off the unwanted associations. A man for example needs to be a member of the aristocracy, or a court photographer, or at least a Saville Row tailor, to bear the name Cecil, and don't ask me to unravel the warp and woof of its history to explain why. Avoid Garth unless the boy weighs 12 pounds at birth, and bear in mind fond parents, that your children are also stuck with a surname (in the male line permanent and inescapable) and that the assonant and visual harmony between the Christian name and the surname is worthy of some thought.

No good calling your son Rock, if your surname is Fish: or your daughter Olive if your family name is Green.

Changing your name by deed poll does of course offer a final bolt hole in escaping from the tyranny of your name - there's no doubt that Archie Leach wasn't going anywhere until he became Cary Grant - but if you take that drastic step make sure it gains you an advantage.

One local bright spark in the *Anchor and Hope* came up with the idea that if you wanted so much a personalised registration plate on your car, don't pay thousands to buy initials as advertised in the national press; buy any old car, which may have the number-plate XOQ, and change your name by deed poll at much less expense to Xerxes Oswald Quigley.

What's in a name after all?

Helpful Hint

A more useful application of the deed poll is to adopt a name with a dozen or more Christian names added . . . While the vicar is saying,

'Do you, Alan George Lionel Frederick Brian Keith William Richard Arthur David Dennis Percival Smith, take this woman . . .' it allows you time in a moment of crisis to change your mind.

As to the dangers of misnaming children, remember the classic verse of Horace.

>*Mr. Snockers a gent from Salonica*
>*Married Norma instead of Veronica*
>*Now poor Norma Snockers*
>*Has to take beta-blockers*
>*To grow tits as described by her monica.*

15. Fringe benefits from the birth of Jesus

Rule 1
Your children are entitled to be introduced to the alternative traditions to atheism.

Rule 2
A tourist to the Holy Land was told that the ferry fare across the Sea of Galilee was £20.

'My goodness,' he exclaimed, 'no wonder Jesus walked.'

Rule 3
The longest running play of all time is the Nativity Play, which has been played millions of times since 1. A.D. Proof that Jesus was not only born again, but again, and again, and again . . .

Personal Case History
There are certain benefits to be derived from raising a family, although we parents have never figured out exactly what they are.

On the disadvantages we can be quite voluble. The duchess, for example, has a large repertoire of cusses in moments of stress ranging from 'Kids? Who'd have them?' and 'Don't let him/her come near me this morning or I'll kill him/her!' to 'I should have ignored my dad and joined the W.R.E.N.S.!' This is a curse based on the wobbly logic that if she had gone into the services during the war, she wouldn't have met me and all the disasters which came with the package.

The joys of parenthood on the other hand are rarely

articulated. Mums and dads are not prone to exclaiming, 'Oh how nice it is to be sitting here surrounded by our children! What a boon they are! What a treasure!' You would have to settle for that silent look of pride, joy, and affection which spreads across your wife's face when she gazes upon her small daughter, all spruced up to go to her first party: much the same look, one imagines, which spread across God's face when he brushed and combed Adam and Eve's hair and walked both of them to their first Paradise.

You have to make the most of fleeting ecstatic moments like that, knowing full well that the next minute your angels will be puffing an experimental fag in the toolshed, or playing mothers and fathers with the kids next door. Alas! the heights of happiness today are too often measured by the tears of sadness in later years, when you realise those days of bliss have gone forever and will never return ... the smiling young faces on the snaps in the family album ... the now empty cot in the small room, which used to keep snug each latest arrival in turn ...

However, I can name one occasion when parents with children are six furlongs ahead of those without, and that is the occasion of the annual local Nativity Play. There's nothing to prevent childless couples attending a Nativity Play of course, but it would be rather like chapel folk paying homage at a Shinto shrine.

The Nativity Play is the only dramatic presentation in the world where every member of the audience has a loved one in the cast on stage. The ritual is unique. In the hallowed story of the birth of the baby Jesus everyone's little precious has been given a part to play, and it doesn't matter how small the part.

'Well where's Freddie then?' whispers the bemused dad scanning the crowded stage.

'He's there at the back,' blubbers his wife, suppressing tears of pride. 'One of the shepherds - oh love him, they've put him in charge of the goat!'

Mothers and fathers who have children with speaking parts, sit in nail-biting torment off the edge of their seats, waiting for the line to be delivered which they have rehearsed over and over again with their offspring all week. And when a small piping voice proclaims 'Behold! I bring you tidings of joy and goodwill...' the inexpressible look of relief, pride and joy that sweeps across their faces is wondrous to behold, scarcely matched by those in the 'Adoration of the Magi' canvas.

Such an atmosphere, charged with the sanctity of the subject, and heavily ionised with the unminced abandon of childlike endeavour, is ready to burst into a thunderclap of humour, as we are rarely let down.

If there is such a thing as *lovely comedy* you will find it in the manger next to the inn. You'll get some clue when half of the children of Israel, draped in their mum's discarded blankets, pay no attention to what is happening on stage and wave front-toothless grins at their various mums and dads. The ritual becomes extended when Mum mouths wordlessly at her son 'Pay attention to Jesus,' and the kid mouths back 'Do what?' It results in half a dozen Israelites conducting a mouthing conversation with their embarrassed parents.

During the growing-up days of my family, I never missed one Nativity Play. A long blank period followed after they became too old, but my patronage was re-vitalised with the arrival of grandchildren.

Just lately we have had some ripping productions well up to scratch Jesus-wise and laughter-wise. Last year our five year-old grandson was only rated shepherd fifth class, but it was enough to stimulate an affectionate tear from the Grand Duchess, and at the same time hit new heights in divine comedy.

The New School of teachers decided that the dialogue would be improvised. The idea was to explain the general role to each main character and then leave it to him or her to make up the dialogue in a natural sort of way. It produced a comedic level that Mel Brooks, Neil Simon, and Woody Allen couldn't have produced working as a group.

'And behold! A star appeared in the East . . .' announced the angel Gabriel.

'Please teacher,' said the Virgin Mary, raising her hand. 'I want to say something.'

Improvisation reached its peak in the exchange between Joseph and the innkeeper.

'There's no room 'ere,' invented the innkeeper. 'We're flup. You'll 'ave to go in the manger.'

'But my wife's pregnant!' improvised an outraged Joseph.

'That's not my fault,' said the innkeeper.

'Well it ain't my fault either,' rejoined Joseph: at once provoking a gale of laughter from the audience and unconsciously dramatising the Immaculate Conception.

This Christmas the local landlord of a popular hostel, and a well known eccentric by the name of Obadiah Roberts, decided to pre-empt the local school's effort and staged a Nativity Play of his own in the dining room and bar of his inn. He obviously scorned Cecil B. de Mille crowd scenes and left-wing leanings towards improvised dialogue, preferring to rely on a small hand-picked cast with the action mimed to his commentary, thus doing away with dialogue altogether. Obadiah's eccentricity was shown in his not bothering to inform his customers, and parties turning up for a quiet evening meal in a country inn found a Nativity Play in progress with the waitresses acting as stage hands.

'**** the customers,' growled Obadiah, who couldn't wait to climb into his Emir's outfit as the commentator.

Probably his interest in his own role caused him to overlook his hand-picked cast, which included an innkeeper who was stone deaf, and Matthew and Thomas my two grandsons, aged 3 and 5. They were admittedly only two lowly shepherds, but nobody had told Obadiah (least of all their mother) that they were accident-prone shepherds.

The stage was set; which was in fact a small open space at the end of the dining room in front of the bar with a stage entrance right (a door) and a stage entrance-or-exit left (a flight of stairs descending to the cellar). Another flight of steps going up was used for an ethereal effect, down which the angel Gabriel appeared. The audience was composed of a small group of sweating parents, including the duchess and my son and daughter-in-law, and several bemused diners studying their menus and trying to find a wine waiter.

Things began rather well. Obadiah, who upon advice had toned down his eastern potentate's outfit to a racy combination of Mahala-al-hashbash and Yasser Arafat, stood discreetly in the shadows and intoned with reverential awe.

'And it came to pass that a star rose in the east, and certain shepherds tending their flocks . . .'

Just for once it looked as if the whole story of the Virgin Mary's confinement and delivery was going to be enacted without a hitch, and even the blighted dining customers stopped looking at the menus for a starter and paid attention to the action. A warning of trouble ahead came with Joseph's knock on the inn door, not heard by the deaf innkeeper, a gangly youth of nine.

'Open it,' hissed Obadiah. The innkeeper didn't hear that either and went on doing innkeeperish things, which consisted mostly of wandering vaguely about flailing his arms up and down.

'Open it!' roared Obadiah, and this the innkeeper heard and opened the door to reveal Joseph and Mary who were actually waiting in the cold outside.

'No room!' screamed the innkeeper and slammed the door.

'Will you let them in!' screamed back Obadiah, and after some confusion the worthy couple were admitted, followed by a donkey for whom a special ramp had been provided. The donkey slid all the way down the ramp and then was immediately conducted by its minder back up again, it having presumably provided the necessary amount of local colour. This was held up by the arrival of another dining party who were not expecting to meet a donkey coming out of their favourite dinery. At this point in Obadiah's version the angel Gabriel appeared down the ethereal steps, a pretty little thing who elicited the required 'Aaah's' from the audience; even though her mother had appeared to have got confused between the angel Gabriel and the Fairy Queen and she looked with her wand and silver paper sparkle as if she had descended from the top of a Christmas tree rather than Heaven. For some reason she struck a balletesque pose over Obadiah's commentary with one toe stuck in the air and totally distracted us from the plot in fear that she might go for a purler down the rest of the stairs.

There was a commotion stage right and the door burst open to admit the Three Wise Men and shepherds various. Matthew led the throng holding a dog by the lead. We worked out that the dog was a stand-in for a goat. Thomas our three year-old, followed precipitately; someone had made the mistake of giving him a walking stick as a shepherd's crook. His entrance was marred by the tangle of the walking stick with his blanket and he fell flat on his face mid-stage. Gales of laughter. I've seen older children burst into tears and run off the stage at such an indignity, but Tombo merely treated his audience with a wide grin, only to be snatched by his mother, who was hiding down the cellar steps (stage left).

Order would have been restored but Matthew's emblematical goat got away, and while various members of the New Testament tried to retrieve him, a walking stick sneaked out from the cellar steps followed by Tombo's face, who made various attempts to trip people up. For a period this whole harlequinade bore no relation to Obadiah's plodding commentary whatsoever, a macabre touch being added by the back-ground music of Nat King Cole singing ballads, further evidence of Obadiah's eccentricity.

Obadiah's commentary got back into synch with the mimodrama, with the myrrh and frankincense scene, although the audience saw little through the tears of spent laughter.

While Tombo was trying to hook his stick round the ankles of the ascended Angel, Matthew stuck grimly to the principle that the show must go on and glared fixedly into the middle distance, ignoring the dog who came back idly wagging its tail. Still, he thought afterwards that it was a jolly good play, and so did Obadiah and so did everybody else. Over a celebratory pint I asked Obadiah why one Wise Man gave Jesus a packet of Wrigleys Spearmint.

'It was the best we could do old horse,' he boomed, 'in place of myrrh, which is an aromatic gum.'

'What could Jesus do with a packet of Wrigleys?' I asked.

'Come to that, what would he do with a dollop of aromatic gum?' roared Obadiah. He patted the innkeeper's head. 'Sorry I shouted at you old son. Did you enjoy the play?'

'What?' said the innkeeper.

Helpful Hint

Mother: Jesus taught us that we are here to help others.
Child: What do the others do?
   Have an answer prepared for this.

16. Pulling out all the plugs

Rule 1
If your electric cooker has a twelve-month guarantee, it means that you can guarantee it will be twelve months before they come and repair it.

Rule 2
A new electrically powered car can travel from London to Manchester for a fraction of the cost of a petrol-driven vehicle. The only snag is that 200 miles of flex...

Rule 3
The dangers of hi-tech development were illustrated in a recent letter to *The Electrical Gazette*.

Dear Sir, Can someone sort out all the radio-controlled gadgetry? I wear a pace-maker and on coming out of the house I saw a young girl pass by with a prominent bouncing bosom. At which point my automatic garage doors opened, my t.v. boomed out, and a vibrator started up in my wife's handbag.

Yours, recently divorced...

Personal Case History
The words a harassed husband wants to hear least are those spoken to me by the duchess yesterday when she said with a certain pleading tone,

'Fix me a plug on my new iron sometime will you?'

She knows it doesn't pay to be peremptory when it comes to matters electrical. As soon as she spots me with a screwdriver and a roll of insulating tape in my hands, she ushers the kids out of the house, opens the windows to let the blue air out, and adopts a low profile until I've finished.

And for good reason. Whereas in every civilised country in the world, every room is liberally fitted with wall-sockets, only in Britain do they condescend to give you one per room. This entails the use of adaptors with wires snaking across the floor like fire hoses across the street during the Blitz.

There are so many adaptors behind our television set, it looks like a madman has been let loose in a Lego factory. There can't be a house in Britain that doesn't rate alongside Windsor Castle as a fire risk. Whereas in every civilised country in the world you can buy an electric toothbrush and find a plug already fitted, only in Britain can you still pay a fortune for a deep-freeze and find three bare wires sticking out the back. And finally, whereas in every civilised country in the world, the electric plug is a neat two-pronged pin, only in Britain do you come across a massive Victorian museum piece which should have gone out with mangles, battleships and commodes.

I would cheerfully give up a month's pay if somebody could explain why we are still lumbered with these monstrosities. For the benefit of all young couples canoodling on their sofas and planning their weddings, let me introduce them to the process of fitting a plug. If they still want to get married afterwards, good luck to them.

First, examine the bare wires of the appliance to be fitted. There are three stubby wires of different colours. None of them is long enough to be fitted into the plug, so the protective plastic covering has to be cut back.

Second. Although every manufacturer knows that the positive and the earth connections have to be longer than the negative connection - because they are positioned at the top of the plug and the negative is at the bottom - just for fun they always leave you with the wires on the appliance cut at equal length. Have you now cut back the negative shorter than the other two? Good. You will now find (as we all do) that it won't reach because you've cut off too much.

Third. Thirty minutes and the same number of swear words later, you come to the electric plug itself.

Unscrew the locking nut and this will enable you to separate the two halves. Commit the internal structure quickly to memory because one touch of the screwdriver will spew the contents on the floor in a shower of metal prongs, screws, fuses and fuse clips. Allow 15 minutes to put all the bits back in their right place.

I could conduct you through the intricacies of trying to wind the end of the wires round the terminals where there is no room to do so, and coping with the fuse that keeps springing out, but I've had enough. Even describing the nightmare is blowing my own fuse.

Just keep your duchess out of the ring until the fight is over. It doesn't help to hear her petulant voice behind you.

'Oh for goodness' sake don't get so bad tempered!'

It took me forty minutes and three large scotches to fix the plug on the iron lead. The lead turned out to be too short to stretch to the ironing board unless it shared a wall-plug with three other appliances. We worked it out that she could iron, boil the kettle, and toast bread at the same time, but that would cut off the phone and obliterate all the stored memory numbers. Or she could keep the phone going, iron, and boil, but forego the toast.

This story illustrates the triumph of the bonds of marriage over the dark forces that have chained us forever to the British electrical system. Now and again even marriage deserves a plug (two-pronged of course).

Helpful Hint

Electrical equipment plays havoc with fuel bills. Forget the electric egg-timer. For a 4½ minute egg sing three verses of Rosie O'Grady. Chuck out the jacuzzi. Get the same effect with a warm bath and slinging six cats in.

17. All My Worldly Goods

Rule 1
In our poor days burglars used to break into our house just for the practice.

Rule 2
When it comes to home protection the Americans work on the principle, *He who lives by the sword can't afford a gun.*

Rule 3
Protect your own home. We all hate being robbed of our possessions; it's not their sentimental value that matters, it's the money.

Personal Case History
'There's something missing,' I said, shaking my head when I came in from work. 'I don't know what it is, but something's missing.'

'Didn't you notice?' exclaimed the duchess. 'Follow me.' She took me to the front door, opened it, and swept an arm over the porch. 'They've gone. Somebody stole them during the night.'

'Our ash trays!' I cried.

'And I know who pinched them,' she nodded.

'You know? Did you phone the police?'

'How could I? I didn't notice they'd gone myself until I opened the door to go shopping. Didn't you notice they were missing? You went out first.'

'No I didn't notice because - you always expect them to be there don't you? It's like the roof. You don't check the roof every morning to see if it's there. But how do you know who's taken them?'

'It's those men isn't it. The ones that keep coming round and asking if we want our front drive done over. They spotted them and have walked off with them.'

'How could they lift them? They're solid cast iron.'

I should explain that *ashtrays* was our pet name for two enormous genuine Victorian flower urns.

'And I had just planted both of them with fresh spring Busy Lizzies,' said the duchess with a sob.

Oh dear duchess, we had just had our first burglary. We reported it to the police of course. Had we a photograph of them for identification purposes? Had we a photograph of them? We hunted through albums and shoeboxes full of old snaps. The only snap we had of one of them was partially obscured by the Grand Duchess standing in front of it.

'Trust your mother to stand in the way of the evidence,' I murmured. I explained to the sergeant. 'Sorry about the mother-in-law, but that big scalloped urn behind her is what they stole.'

'I bet you wish they'd stole the mother-in-law,' quipped the sergeant.

We never saw the ashtrays again. The duchess is far more sensitive about losing material possessions than I am. I suffer from a momentary pang of anger and then shake it off, but the duchess gets herself upset for days. Even today, I try not to mention ashtrays, even when I am referring to ashtrays. Later that day when she opened the family committee meeting, which she usually does as she gets into bed and stares at the ceiling, she said,

'You know we ought to start to think about looking after our property more than we do - especially when we go on holiday.'

This was true. We were brought up in the days when mums left their front doors open, drivers left their cars unlocked, bikes were propped up unchained in the kerb, bank clerks counted your cash over an open counter, and the only people you were likely to come across down a dark lane were kissing couples.

'But it's a bit like closing the stable door after the horses have bolted,' I observed.

'They didn't bolt. They were carted off by two brawny men,' she retorted. 'And there's plenty more in the stable to pinch if they have a mind to paying us another visit - or any other burglar.'

Operation *Lock Up* was put into motion prior to our going on holiday. The duchess warned all the neighbours and provided our date of departure and date of return. Our next door neighbour was given our key and asked to clear tell-tale build-ups of mail away from the front door. For no reason at all I began to feel intimations of doom. I don't know why. Perhaps it's because one hears stories from time to time which prove that real life goes contrary to the sanctimoniousness of Aesop's moralising, and that it is very often those who take the most meticulous caution and the wisest decisions who are the very ones who fate rewards with a whack in the crutch.

I recalled a story about a variety magician who always rigged his house with hidden trip wires, man traps, leaping ghosts, and falling objects, before leaving his house for a prolonged engagement. On returning he made his wife stand by the gate before he deactivated all his devilish booby traps. Then he remembered just too late as he entered the front door that he had rigged a beam to drop as it was opened . . . The duchess interrupted my thoughts.

'Now we have to put all the expensive things away,' she said.

'Where?'

'We'll have to find safe hiding places of course. We can't leave them about for burglars to come in and help themselves.'

The first few minutes were easy, although we did have a difference of opinion on what was a hiding place.

'You can't put the Lladro in there,' protested the duchess as I opened her needlework box.

'Why not?' I countered.

'It takes me hours to find anything in there. It's a jungle.'

Then we started to argue about what was valuable.

'You're not going to hide mother's clock are you?' I bleated.

'Keep your voice down!' whispered she (the Grand Duchess had ears like Jodrell Bank). 'It's her wedding present and she'd never forgive me if it was stolen.'

'I was going to leave it out and hope it would be,' I said.

As the operation proceeded, the duchess' concept of what was valuable in the house expanded to include presents from Shanklin, chipped wine glasses, and a porcelain moose with his left antler missing. The rooms began to look bare and the hiding places began to run out.

'If we go on at this rate,' I complained, 'the hiding places will become more obvious than the ordinary places and we'll have to use the ordinary places as hiding places.'

'I'm not taking my valuable jewellery,' said the duchess coming to a decision. I'll just take my cheap and cheerful costume jewellery and hide the valuable away. Or will it be safer to take it with me?'

She gazed at me for a decision.

'Why don't you hide your big diamond ring,' I suggested. 'And take the rest, then if you lose any of it on holiday, at least you wouldn't have lost all of it.'

This compromise seemed to satisfy her and she selected her most precious stone and went into a brown study as to where to hide it.

On our return from the holiday, tanned and weary, the children shot off in different directions, knowing it would take their mother at least two hours de-securing the home before she got around to putting them to bed. All looked well. Nobody had stolen the roof or the front garden. I reconnected the car battery. The duchess reclaimed the key and informed the neighbours of our return and enquired if there had been any emergencies. Only one: our freezer had broken down but our neighbour had rescued the food and put it in her own.

Over the next few days we gradually retrieved our *objets d'art* from their hiding places and replaced them in their usual positions. It seemed that our first Operation *Lock Up* was a success.

Several days later the duchess confided,

'I can't find my ring.'

'You mean - *the* ring?' I gasped.

'I hid it somewhere, but I can't think where.'

'You mean you remembered where you hid your mother's clock,' I said, glancing at the monstrosity on the mantelpiece, 'and you've forgotten where you've hidden the most valuable object in the house?'

This was most uncharacteristic of the duchess. She is one of nature's squirrels. She never throws a thing away. Months, even years later, I will ask 'Where's that old magnifying glass of your father's we used to have?' or some such object, and she will know exactly where it is and retrieve it. On the other hand I did read in one of those 'I-bet-you-didn't-know-this' articles which abound in the *Reader's Digest*, that contrary to popular belief, squirrels bury nuts and then forget where they've buried them.

The next few weeks were tragic for the duchess, and her wheels gradually began to drop off one by one as she went through the daily torture of overcoming her anger and frustration and stirring her memory at the same time.

Each evening I returned from work I went through a series of suggestions with her as to where she might have hidden it.

'How about inside the chandelier? Tucked between tissues

in a Kleenex box? Buried in a pot of face cream? Tied to a piece of string and dangled down a drain? Screwed inside an electric plug? No?' It was like playing twenty questions when even the quiz master doesn't know the answer. 'Can't you remember *anything* about it? Whether it was upstairs or downstairs - in the kitchen - the garden shed?'

'Oh stop it,' sighed the duchess. 'You're only confusing me more.'

'It looks as if you had a complete blackout to me,' I said. 'You could have gone out and robbed a bank that day and not known about it. So cheer up, you might come across a big sack of hidden money one day.'

She threw me a warning look. A small six year-old reading Rupert Bear piped into her pages,

'Maybe you forgot to hide it at all, and it's still in your jewellery box?'

The duchess gasped and shot upstairs. It would have been a perfect end to the story but life ain't like that and no ring was nestling coyly in a red velvet bed.

The news gradually spread among friends and relations and soon our whole social circle was on tenterhooks about the fate of the lost object. It was the first question asked at parties and get-togethers. Attending the funeral of a social acquaintance we spotted an old friend in the congregation; she smiled and silently mouthed, 'Have you found it yet?' whilst miming putting a ring on a finger. The vicar was in the middle of that bit about 'Man that is born of a woman hath but a short time to live . . .' and by the look he threw her I would have given her about five minutes. She had the grace to apologise afterwards at the funeral breakfast.

'My friend here has lost her ring.'

The vicar smiled wanly.

'I've heard of rings lost at weddings many times,' he uttered, 'but never at funerals.'

The duchess was reluctant to claim the insurance.

'I won't get half the value of it because it required a special premium which I didn't take out. And I know I shall remember where I put it some day. I'm bound to come across it.'

But she didn't come across it, or even a stack of bank notes. As time passed by, the heartache of the vanished valuable retreated into the background, only to hang over us, like a black cloud on the horizon of a blue sky, like a nagging embarrassment from some social brick one dropped many years ago, or a patch of skin irritation that rages when one's spirits are low. Off and on, I found myself idly lifting the lid of the loo cistern, up-ending old shoes, feeling inside decayed vases and pots in the shed, and upon a casual thought, up-turning the odds-and-ends jar, which contains every nick-nack we don't want to throw away and never use. No diamond ring.

A year went by. Was it two? I was slumped in my favourite chair trying to re-charge my batteries watching the third repeat of a repeat of a BBC situation comedy which wasn't funny in the first place, when the duchess strode in with a serene smile on her face. It was the sort of look that Giotto would have painted on the face of the mother when the prodigal son returned. In her hand she brandished a bright diamond ring. Perhaps the comparison is not ill-fitting. Wasn't the prodigal son given a robe and shoes and a ring to put on his finger? Next to the ecstasy of the return of a long-lost loved one is the joy on the rediscovery of a family heirloom long since thought gone for ever. Oh the relief! the pleasure of re-possession! which has nothing to do with its price.

'I was sorting out some old dresses for Oxfam,' explained the duchess breathlessly, 'and feeling in the pockets as I usually do, when I came across it. Wasn't that lucky! I was about to throw the darn dress away.'

I was relieved because she was relieved, overjoyed because

she was overjoyed. I didn't question the tortuous mental process that prompted her to hide the ring in the pocket of an old dress screwed up in a box, although confessedly it wasn't the first place a burglar would look.

'Next time,' I suggested, 'you tell me where you hide valuables so that you've got a fail-safe memory bank if you forget again.'

She thought so much of my memory that going on subsequent holidays she ignored me and told her hiding places to our daughter-in-law Rosie. Sometimes visitors to Rosie's stare puzzled at her telephone pad and comment,

'That's an odd name.'

'What?'

'Shower Pipe. You've got a note here *Ring up Shower Pipe*.'

Helpful Hint

If you are obliged to leave your house unattended for a lengthy period, before leaving, very carefully choreograph your furniture to make it look as if the house has been ransacked. (Slashing out the middle of an old unwanted oil-painting is an added nice touch). Hopefully a burglar on entering will assume your place has already been *done*.

18. The re-patter of tiny feet

Rule 1
It is written in The Table of Kindred in the Book of Common Prayer that *a man may not marry his grandmother.*

Make sure your wife puts her grandson straight on that matter as there is obviously a lot of that going on.

Rule 2
A sobering thought:

Think upon your grandparents; you loved them but they were not important in your lives.

(Tibetan Proverb)

Rule 3
The small girl strode into the neighbour's lounge which had just been redecorated and looked around critically. The neighbours waited for her comment.

'Well *I* don't think it looks ghastly,' she said, and strode out.

Moral: grandparents sometimes forget not to say things in front of small children.

Personal Case History
The arrival of grandchildren in a family is always a joyous event. Well, for most of the time. There is of course the psychological shock of suddenly being called *Grandpa*, which is easily absorbed when it is used by the grandchildren themselves. It is only when your own wife starts liberally sprinkling *Grandpa's* all around the house that your ego starts to suffer a bruising.

You're probably like me; you still fondly nurse the

illusion that you are your duchess's White Knight, that dashing athletic beau she fell in love with in days of derring-do. After a few 'Ask your Grandpa to put your shoes on', 'Grandpa will play the game with you', and 'Go out in the garden with Grandpa', you get the message that she no longer sees you as an Olympic contender but as an old man with a stick. A prolonged session with the grandchildren induces senility. You find yourself cancelling the weekend golf in case you have an embarrassing attack of something on the tenth tee. Your love-life takes a sharp plunge, with visions of your body imploding like a de-boned chicken under the stress of the act.

The other thing you discover is that looking after the grandchildren for a day is quite a different thing from looking after them for a week. In the weekly version, all the agonies of rearing the young, which you have long forgotten, are like the re-opening of healed scars. Sleepless nights over crying sessions, and trying to remember in vain the symptoms of measles, mumps, and chicken-pox; dealing with sulks and refusals to eat, marvelling at the way the small can be sick at the drop of a hat, and coping with unannounced rear-end explosions.

Even the duchess, as she flops thankfully into bed, mutters,

'My God, we must have been fit to have brought up our brood!'

It's rather like going through a time-warp and having your life put back thirty years, with only half the energy to live it.

We have be reintroduced to the old disciplines: like whispering after the children's bedtime, turning down the television set, and switching off lights before opening doors. As a young father I recall whispering as soon as I returned from work. For ten years the duchess and I didn't have a conversation indoors in a normal voice. One became brainwashed. After 6.30 pm I automatically started whispering. I found myself ordering dinners in hotels in whispers. After a while the waiters were whispering back. As for the lights, the veil of Morpheus is very thin with two year-olds. A glow worm can wake them from a deep sleep into full cry. Hence the routine for switching off lights. On one occasion I inadvertently switched off the light in a men's toilet before exiting, leaving three men fumbling in the dark. It was pure habit.

Yes, there are certain penalties to be paid for hearing once again the patter of tiny feet on the landing: getting used to wiping runny noses, forcing aged enthusiasms to get excited over tiddly-winks, remembering to keep all breakables out of grabbing reach, avoiding tripping over building blocks, and not least dragging the mind away from self-indulgent habits and pre-occupations to give the infants the constant attention they demand.

Nevertheless, I would advocate to all those who are trying to stay married to suffer little grandchildren to come unto them. There is something inexpressibly endearing about the way they squirm onto your lap clutching a favourite book, eager to be read to.

You will discover that you have a very special relationship with your grandchildren that you will not find with anyone else in the world. And if, as you start reading *Once upon a time there was a poor little ugly duckling* you start to feel a warm wet patch spread over your lap, tell yourself never mind - their mum and dad are coming to fetch them tomorrow.

Helpful Hint

Hang on to that old pair of trousers you thought of throwing away.

19. The Keeper of the Purse

Rule 1
'You don't realise the cost of running this house. I'm breaking into £5 notes every minute when I go out. Tomorrow it will be £10 notes.'

'Don't go out tomorrow.'

Rule 2
Are you spending too much? Look at it this way: if you lived your life all over again you probably couldn't afford it.

Rule 3
Marry the type of wife who says to the shop assistant, 'I'm not paying all this money for a toilet cleaner that claims to kill 'all known germs'. I want one that kills the unknown ones as well.'

Personal Case History
I recall the occasion when my cook, house-maid, gardener, nanny, and housekeeper, all departed at the same time and left me in the lurch: in other words the duchess had a spell in hospital. (For one of those things ending in -ectomy).

I coped as best as I could looking after the the family. I shall leave out the majority of my problems including my ignorance of cooking. (I couldn't keep phoning up the duchess in hospital just to ask how long one cooks Brussels sprouts, so I sought help from Cynthia Penfold next door. All that taught me was the she couldn't cook either, which probably explained the permanent pinched look on Arthur's face.)

No, I concentrate on the problems of running the housekeeping purse, and here I should say that figure-work is not my strong point. In 'matric' I only scraped through with a dodgy 'pass'. Given one of those algebraic problems like 'If it takes four men to dig an acre in five days, how many men will it take to dig three acres in six days?' I could never work out what to call 'X' in the first place to start the whole equation going. My inadequacy merely caused me to laugh at the ludicrousness of the problem. How do you know if the second lot of men are going to work as hard as the first lot? And given that they had to dig three acres in six days, wouldn't N.U.P.E. or some such union call them out on strike for being put to work without any pay?

In his end-of-term report my maths teacher compared teaching me maths to trying to bang a nail into steel with a stalk of cooked asparagus.

In any case, I soon discovered that dexterity with figures was only a minor requirement in running the household budget. An iron discipline in expenditure and unwavering policy of putting financial prudence before pleasure was paramount. I began to appreciate the duchess's talents.

I couldn't hope to match her knowledge of all the comparative prices in the supermarkets and her keen nose for sniffing a bargain or a 'special'; consequently I spent so much over the odds that I had to borrow money from myself to make up the deficit.

I left the incoming bills alone, lacking her diligence in questioning every phone call on the telephone bill, and every item on the credit card account, in checking the gas and electrical charges against our meter readings, and her infinite knowledge derived from many years of deep research into car insurance quotes, building society loans, public utility maintenance contracts, and cut-price holiday bargains. In the process of paying in received income, I likewise lacked her expertise in juggling deposit accounts with savings and 'special' accounts, which she did with the infinite ease of a trick-cyclist playing a violin on a tight-rope, thus steering our fiscal boat between the Scylla of extravagance and the Charybdis of buying a pig-in-a-poke.

As I struggled with the day's menu, wondering if there was a sixth way of cooking eggs other than boiled, fried, scrambled, poached, and omeletted, I slowly began to realise how advanced the duchess's experience in the sub-culture of household economy was. Long before the word ecology was ever thought of, she was reprocessing old curtains into new chair-backs, old long trousers into new shorts, old outer nappies into new hand towels, and old hand towels into new polishing rags. Although today she has as deep an appreciation of luxury as the next woman, she has her own scale of values. One evening dining-out equals two pairs of new shoes for the boys. Two tickets to the annual club dance equals a badly needed new tyre for the car. A purchase of chocolates and sweets equals two days supply of fresh vegetables, and so on.

Dear bride and groom, as I raise a metaphorical glass to toast your future happiness, let me explain that the object of this eulogy of my wife's talents is to demonstrate that the man of the household is not necessarily the better keeper of the purse, and make a plea for you to put aside your macho-male and women's-lib pride, and hand the purse over to the partner who has the knack and the dedication.

But before you clamber into your honeymoon car and rattle off dragging your tin cans behind you, let me, like the Ancient Mariner, hold you with my glittering eye and tell you of the stormy financial seas you are about to cross.

You are indeed fortunate, for despite my early divorce from mathematics and lack of cunning in the world of the special bargain and '5p Off', I am an old salt when it comes to sailing the fiscal seas, and can spot a storm or a rip tide or a hidden rock before it is coming.

The first thing you will notice, as you come to grips with your wall-to-wall mortgage and quarterly bills is that prices go up by the lift, and your income goes up by the stairs, and not all the love in the world, with the combined aid of Venus, Eros, and Aphrodite, can make up the difference. You can hump each other three times a night and breath words of undying love, but it doesn't bring down the price of a cabbage.

This incredibility gap is known as 'the cost of living', and as everybody knows the cost of living always goes up and never goes down. In fact the cost of living has been going up since 3000 BC when the Pharoahs started building the Pyramids, and except for a brief period when the Goths and Visigoths gobbled up civilisation for a few hundred years, it has been going up ever since, and is destined to go up for the next five millenia; so newly-weds, put that into your post office savings book and smoke it.

But why does it go up? Oh hasn't anybody explained that to you? (The reason is that not even the most brain-loaded Treasury expert knows why.) The only person in the world who can explain it to you is me. So aren't you lucky to be reading this book? Mind you, it won't bring down the price of a cabbage, but if it eases your mind to know why you can't afford a summer holiday on the Costa Bomb this year, I will explain why.

Did I mention the Pyramids? Yes I did. You may have wondered in your idle moments, whilst pouring sand onto your navel sunbathing on the beach, or scraping the gunge off the blades of your hedge-clippers, why the Pyramids were built in the shape they were. As far as I know that fundamental question has never been asked or answered. As containers of royal tombs, square blocks or cylinders would have been more commodious. But that wouldn't have pleased the Pharaohs.

It so happened that the pyramid so exquisitely expressed in stone the shape of Egyptian society at the time. Its massive slave population formed the base, and it ascended in ever shortening strata of rank and privilege up to His Most Eminent Potentate the Pharaoh Cheops at the very tip.

We can be assured that by the time a slave had carried his share of the ninety million cubic tons of stone higher and higher until his particular pyramid had been completed, he had been reminded in terms of physical effort (if he ever lived that long) of his place in the scheme of things and just how difficult it was to ascend the social hierarchy. The pyramids in other words, were not merely monuments to the omnipotence of the Pharaoh Kings, they were early exercises in brain-washing by hard labour.

Four thousand and a bit years later, the pyramidal structure of a society was still popular: it was the matrix of every society in medieval Europe. The king was at the top and the serfs and villeins were on the bottom, with the nobility, the clergy, the craftsmen and the merchants all slotting neatly into their alloted place in the tapering edifice.

Nevertheless, and it is the biggest nevertheless in history, the story of mankind has been the story of his slowly turning the pyramid into an oblong. The process is as undetectable as the growth of a stalagmite, but it is inexorable, unstoppable. Like the salmon inspired to struggle upstream to spawn, man is ineluctably possessed by a demon to struggle upwards and better his position. Call it ambition, call it 'making something of your life', only a few start at the bottom and stay there because they like it.

Slaves struggle for their freedom and for a basic wage. Peasants fight for land. Fishermen and farmers seek for greater recompense. One class is forever fumbling for a foothold in the class above it. That is why corporals seek to become sergeants, why rent-payers buy their council houses, and call their sons Jason when they used to call them Charlie.

As the bulge moves further up the pyramid, powers and dominions totter, and the great lords of the land have to open their houses to the public at £5 a ticket.

Now the very tips of the pyramids - the presidents, the Chairmen, the dictators and generals, are regularly removed to make way for the next one coming up. Kingdoms have robbed their kings and queens of all real power. (Our own has reached the stage of telling its royalty to pay its whack, or else).

(My patient bride and groom, hear me out, you have plenty of time to get to Gatwick).

But there is a price to pay. Every time a slave moves into the stratum of paid worker, all those above have to provide the money. With each migration of the native out of the wastelands, the deserts, and the forests into the factory, the cost of a newspaper mysteriously climbs by a couple of pence, and Sainsburys sneak an extra sixpence on their tomatoes. With the world's population increasing at a tremendous rate, and being sucked into the induction end of the pyramid, the cost of merely maintaining one's status in the tottering structure will be daunting enough.

(You don't mind if I come in your car to Gatwick do you? I haven't quite finished.)

So much for the vast anthropogenesis of man and its powerful (and expensive) tidal sweep of which your dream boat is subject.

You are also sailing on the cross-currents of the world economy. The world economy is extremely simple to understand - whenever there is a crisis the price of a loaf of bread goes up.

It doesn't matter if it happens to be the fears arising from the collapse of peace talks in the Middle East, the failure of the rice harvest in Trichinopoly, the fall of the dollar against the yen, or what new cabinet scandal is revealed by *The Sun*, the celerity with which it hits the loaf is wondrous. Remember that all crises are sudden, and therefore all changes in the value of your money are sudden. Just as you have paid the final instalment on your washing machine, paid the £14.50 to the *Readers Digest* for the copies you didn't ask for, made the first down-payment on a video machine, contributed to the enormous concentration of wealth among plumbers by paying £50 to your own for a five minute visit, and are thinking of dropping a speculatory coin in the pub fruit machine - someone announces that 'the price of petrol will go up by 10p as from tomorrow.'

(Don't go through Immigration just yet, I'm nearly through.)

Have I any tips as a veteran married man to help you make ends meet? Yes of course. Basically, don't live in Britain. It is the most advanced country in the world - the first officially to give up work. It is only logical. Our country was the first to introduce the Industrial Revolution, and it is the first to do away with it. We can't shed our coal, steel, shipbuilding, fishing and cotton industries quick enough in our precipitous dash to the nearest Leisure Centre. The computers may be a bit late in taking over, but by golly when they do, we won't be neurotic workaholics like the Yanks, Germans and Japs. We've had more practice at doing nothing than anybody. It's nice to be more civilised than anyone else, but let's face it, can you ever remember when this country was rich? Since the day I was born I seem to recall that we've been forever exhorted to tighten our belts, export or die, save power, in a long procession of depressions, recessions, devaluations, currency restrictions, power cuts, cancellations, redundancies, three-day weeks, production cut-backs, and financial collapses. It's terribly miserable being the most advanced country in the world. I leave the choice to you.

(There's still plenty of time before your plane leaves: why don't you visit the Duty Free shop and buy something? No? Was it something I said?)

Helpful Hint

How to send letters free: do not affix a stamp. Address the letter to a non-existent name and location. On the back write *if undelivered return to . . .* together with the name and address of your intended recipient.

20. On getting lost

Rule 1
In the old days mothers used to pour syrup-of-figs, sennapods, and castor oil down their kids' throats. They didn't know whether or not it improved their health, but they always knew where to find them.

Rule 2
If inadvertently caught, whilst driving in the inner-city traffic system of any British town, think positive. Tie a ball of wool to your rear bumper and knit yourself a pullover while trying to find the way out.

Rule 3
Sometimes a marriage *gets lost*. In such a case sit down and discuss matters with your spouse coolly and rationally, even if the discussion gets so loud the police call in.

Personal Case History
I've been thinking hard lately (so I can forewarn starry-eyed lovers who are determined to tie the knot) of instances in the past where the duchess and I always lose our cool and a giant jemmy threatens to prize open the nuptial padlock. Our long-time friends Freda and George are constantly *falling out* and the number of times her suitcase has been packed and dumped by the front door is only slightly less than the number of hot dinners she has cooked. Mabel and Freddy sleep in separate rooms. When Mary and Joe fall out, Mary goes on a spending spree. Doris and Edgar have a built-in shock absorber to cushion marital spats in the way of cats. Edgar hates cats, and Doris always has at least two. When

things are going badly she takes in another couple. Every marriage has some sort of safety-valve to let off excess conjugal steam, and ours is when we are in the car.

Good, because I think I'm on common ground here. There aren't many friends' cars one can travel in without hearing the familiar litany: 'Don't drive so fast'. 'Are you wearing the right glasses?' 'Sort them out dear.' 'We do have another gear for going up hills sweetheart.' 'Don't do that when you take your test dear - you'll never pass.' And other such sarcasms, from one spouse or another, whoever happens to be at the wheel. The duchess and I go through this ritual more or less as soon as the car inches forward out of the driveway. (To be honest she is a better driver than I am when it comes to saving pounds sterling off the insurance premium, but I am equal to saving lives in an emergency).

Somehow tempers always reach boiling point whenever we take the wrong turning, or get lost. At such a point I do my best to remember that the natural skills of the male and female are complementary rather than equal and competitive. A newspaper recently printed the results of a mathematical test which proved that women are quicker and more accurate at figure work, but men are more adept at spatial and dimensional problems.

This must explain why the duchess is better than I at balancing the household budget, but her attempts to back the car out of the garage look as if she is trying to dock the QE2 in the Serpentine.

When it comes to locating the position of one's body on the surface of the planet she gives up the ghost altogether. If the duchess had been Captain Cook, Norway would now be called Australia. Only last year she heard some store advertising on the radio an article she wanted, and recruited me as a chauffeur. After driving round for half an hour I said,

'Do you realise, we are looking for a store whose name

you don't know, and even if you did, you don't know where it is?'

'Yes, but it's got to be around here somewhere,' was her answer.

I am no Vasco da Gama, but given a clear night I know one can find the North Star from the Plough, that one can always tell roughly what direction one is going by the position of the sun, and that when one takes a wrong turning or gets lost, the first thing one does is stop and consult a map.

Not so the duchess. She drives blithely on in the naive hope that an elf is going to jump on the bonnet shouting 'Follow me and I'll put you back on the right road!' Petulance, anger, indignation, and rage reverberate between us on these occasions; not divorce but murder threatens especially when we are mapless.

'Why are you driving on and on dear, when you know we are lost and might be going in the wrong direction?'

'Oh be quiet. I'm waiting for the next sign to come up, at least it will tell us where we are. There's one coming up on the left now - what does it say?'

'Welcome to Bath.'

'There you are. At least we know we're in Bath.'

'But we want to go to Taunton. I told you to keep the sun on your left.'

'What at night? There isn't any sun.'

'There was when you first got lost.'

... And so on.

I should have guessed that the car would be our constant battleground from a warning I was given early on in our married life when we went on a rally. During the epoch after the war when folk gradually began to make enough of the necessary to afford a car, weekend rallies enjoyed a brief but enthusiastic popularity. The duchess had not by that time taken her driving test and was cast automatically in the role of navigator whilst I coped with the narrow country lanes of Kent.

The art of map-reading consists in being able to point to the map and say, 'That's where we are'. Thereafter the minor problem of working out the route to one's destination is a doddle. The duchess suffered from what the experts call 'inverse orientation', which means getting into a bit of a two and eight about relating the map to the world outside the car window. She could point to the map and say, 'This is where we ought to be but we aren't' but this isn't much help to the driver who wants to know the direction he should take.

Following several explosive arguments at the start, which obliged me to drive at suicidal speed through Cranbrook and Lamberhurst to make up for loss time, a new note of confidence came into the duchess's voice.

'I've just solved the first clue,' she announced. 'We have to collect a skein of red wool in an old farmhouse.'

'O.K. fine,' I said, slowing down. 'Which way do we go?'

'The farmhouse is *there*,' she replied, thrusting the Ordnance Survey No. 188 in front of my driving nose.

'Take it away! Don't tell me. I'm the driver,' I yelped. 'Tell me how to get there.'

'Oh. Well where are we now?'

'You ought to know that! You're the navigator.' I pulled the car into the side of a dodgy narrow lane and prodded the map.

'We are - *here*. And we've got to get to - *there*. So you call out the turnings I have to make as we go along.'

I started the car. After a pause the duchess told me to turn left.

'We can't possibly turn left,' I said. 'The farmhouse is way over there to the right.'

'Oh. Well if you know where it is, why don't you just drive there?'

'I don't know where it is. I'm only going by the map.' I

prodded the map on her lap with my left hand. 'The map shows it's over to the right from where we started.'

There was a long pause.

'Oh I see,' breathed the duchess, the light of discovery descending upon her, or so I thought. 'In that case you need to turn - er - right, and go through this village.'

I turned right, and drove on.

'There's no village here,' I said.

'Yes there is,' contradicted the duchess staring at the map. 'It's right here - look.'

'**Don't** keep holding it in front of my face! I can't see where I'm going.'

'Sorry. Anyway you should come to a T-junction next.'

'It's not a T-junction,' I observed as we approached nearer. 'It's a fork.'

'Does it matter? Take the left fork and slow down a bit because there's a little alleyway on the right. There it is! Turn down there. And - stop the car!'

'I've got to. There's a haystack in the way.'

The duchess studied the map for a few seconds and then rolled her window down and looked all around.

'Well?' I asked.

She turned to me and shrugged.

'Well here we are, so what's happened to the farmhouse?'

'Nothing has happened to the farmhouse.'

'Well it's not here, so they must have knocked it down, and the map is out of date.'

'Ken Simpson put all the clues in place last night dear. They couldn't have knocked down a farmhouse and built a haystack in its place in twelve hours. Not British workmen.'

'Then wherever he's put the red wool, he's marked it wrong on the map.'

I snatched the map from her.

'Doesn't it occur to you that *you* have made the mistake and misread the map? There is the farmhouse,' I prodded the map, '*there*. But you've taken me somewhere else.'

'Where?'

'How do I know?'

'Well if you can't read a map either, don't blame me.'

We arrived at the pub for the lunchtime rendezvous two hours late and the lunch had finished and the bar had closed. The rally secretary was draining his last pint.

'Didn't you get any clues at all?' he asked, astonished. The duchess offered him a solitary yarn of red wool.

'Oh we scrubbed round that clue,' said the secretary. 'Ken marked the clue on the wrong place on the map. Bad luck.'

I drove home in silence. Later that week whilst at work my red sweater for some odd reason started to unravel from the bottom up.

Helpful Hint

Remember, there are cars with special bucket seats if your wife develops a big bucket.

21. Keeping up with the Joneses

Rule 1
Avoid living near anyone called Jones.

Rule 2
Remember the Joneses have nightmares too - of attending a celebrity affair at which they are the only ones they don't know!

Rule 3
The Joneses are those people who always have to be so annoyingly different! They only go to private functions, they live in a private road, they send their children to private schools, when Mrs Jones has an operation she always *goes private*; and when they make love they begin by fondling each other's public parts.

Personal Case History
I confess to a touch of male piggery on this subject because *keeping up with the Joneses* is a demon which possesses the female soul by and large with the husband reluctantly tagging along. Every married couple at one time or another keeps up with the Joneses and a paper on the subject should form part of any curriculum encouraging them to stay married. The Joneses may not necessarily be found under one roof. For example the wife might take a shine to the cork flooring installed by Mr. and Mrs. A., the new infra-red operated garage door fitted by Mr. and Mrs. B., and the latest dishwasher purchased by Mr. and Mrs. C.; but collectively they represent the Joneses up with whom the wife wants to keep.

The process is by now so well known that it has become enshrined as a cliché in every situation-comedy since *I Love Lucy*.

The wife spots something the Joneses have acquired and immediately starts bullying her husband to acquire the same. The situation develops when the wife goes into the Jones's and tells them what to buy next so that by the same bullying process she can get it too.

'I would feel nervous with all these very expensive possessions you have in the home,' she will say to Mrs Jones innocently. 'I would install that wonderful new house-alarm system they're advertising.' You can guess the rest of the story.

This short preamble is written only to warn fellow male pigs (a) not to keep up with the Joneses, and what is far worse (b) not to become the Joneses themselves, and thus go bankrupt as pacesetters.

I am more interested in relating an incident that occurred to the duchess in this connection.

It so happens that we do have a Joneses under one roof, although not our neighbours. Our Joneses are the separating Nigel and Diedre (the names have been changed to protect us from the guilty). They are of course magnificent snobs. It is widely known that when you go to dinner at Nigel and Diedre's, the conversation will turn to the twee hinterland of art, literature, gourmet living, and the like. Nigel has a beautiful throw-away style in snobbishness you can't help but admire.

Serving you a diminutive sherry as you sit on his genuine but very hard Regency sofa, he will chortle and say breezily,

'Do you read any of Humphrey Leclerc? He's the new art critic in the *Guardian*. Diedre and I can't leave him out ... anyway...', thus immediately putting you in the Philistine tabloid class for the rest of the evening.

Prompted by Diedre, he will launch into long anecdotes

which are no more than vehicles for a stream of parentheses exhibiting his trendy knowledge.

'So there we were in the south of France in this terrible old banger, and Diedre wanted to call in at Valloris. Well you know what Valloris is like (chortle) . . . full of cheap French pottery except for the odd piece of Picasso if you can spot it . . . and on the way we saw a vineyard with the name of this (chortle) wonderful wine we'd had at - where was it Diedre?'

'At the Aldenburgh Festival, wasn't it?'

'Oh yes of course. This (chortle) wonderful wine - not quite a claret - which we just couldn't trace or buy anywhere. Anyway . . .'

And so on. They raided the Sunday supplements for outré subjects.

Unlike a new Porsche or a state-of-the-art home computer, Nigel and Diedre's dialogue was not a possession that your wife hungered to install in her own home. They were Joneses who had a possession that was permanently upmarket and proof against theft, state of the art conversation.

The duchess is a sensible and practical woman but in the conversations at Nigel and Diedre's she is slightly out of her depth. She has a strong suspicion that Nigel and Diedre get a secret pleasure out of knowing it.

Came the time when the duchess was invited to one of their soirées when I was on business abroad. The company was reinforced with a couple with a vague art show-business background, and the conversation, as the duchess reported to me, became rarefied. It was centred on the concept of worthwhile value.

'Well, quite frankly,' confessed the other wife, 'when our baby was born, Robin and I had a long discussion on what to buy, which would be of greater value to the child in the long run - a baby's educational crêche or a Rodin.'

'Oh quite,' said Nigel smoothly. 'It's a hard choice between the practical and the aesthetic advantage to the child . . .'

At this point in relating the incident, the duchess hunched up and emitted a little squeak.

'Oh was I so glad I bit my lip!' she quavered. 'I was just about to say, "Well I'd buy the Rodin. A car's so useful with a new baby".' She laughed until the tears flowed. 'I thought this damn Rodin they kept talking about was a new make of car.'

Perhaps the moral is - don't try and keep up with the Joneses, even with their conversation.

Helpful Hint

Getting one up on the Joneses . . . Make the wife wear her fur coat when she cleans the front step.

22. Spanish according to Mr. Doust

Rule 1
A travelling tip: *When in Rome, do as the Americans, Germans, and Japanese do.*

Rule 2
A traveller complained to his tourist agency that he wasn't warned that it was vital to know the rudiments of the language of the country he visited. In the Far East a maiden gabbled to him incomprehensively, took him to a room, and engaged him in sexual intercourse.

'If I had known some basic words,' he said, 'I would have told her I don't go in for that sort of thing.'

Rule 3
Something nearly always gets lost in the translation - usually the luggage.

Personal Case History
'I think we ought to invest in a Spanish phrase book,' considered the duchess on the occasion of our first planned holiday to the land of vino tinto and maraccas. This was many moons ago when we had broken our backs on the mortgage, raised two child allowances, and paid enough tax to buy a nuclear submarine.

'Good idea,' I said, not knowing who was going to make use of it. This was our first Big Break and I had secret plans to see Spain over the edge of a cocktail glass and not go in for a language course. Nevertheless I noticed that the slim volume *A Handbook of Spanish Phrases* by one Mr. Dudley Doust was packed into *my* suitcase. (Young husbands have to learn quickly that when the wife says *we* instead of *I* she means *you*.)

Apart from the phrase book (because we had elected to go to a villa) my case also contained a tin of butter, a jar of marmite, two boxes of tissues, a left-handed potato-peeler, several slabs of chocolate, and enough anti-diarrhoea pills to seal a hole in the Hoover dam. *Just in case* as the duchess put it - the case being mine. Later years proved to me that when the British *get away from it all*, they take half of it with them.

It was in those early tourist days when prop-jobs dumped you in mid-France and you went the rest of the way by coach; when Spanish beaches were innocent of concrete jungles, and the all-paper currency left you with a pocketful of 1-peseta notes which at the end of the day looked like the rag you keep in the car to clean the windscreen.

The villa also came with a maid, because she was hireable for a similar bundle of 1-peseta notes. Nowadays the maids own the villas.

'Well ask her her name,' prompted the duchess blithely. 'You've got the book.' She laid a stress on *You've* as if to suggest we had fought over its possession. 'Oh and tell her dear, that she can have today off while I unpack and put things away, and she can come back tomorrow.'

'Would you like me to give her a summing up of this week in the House of Commons while I am at it?' I offered. 'This is a phrase book I have here, not a pocket interpreter.'

Our two kids, sensing a good row, delayed plans to explore the beach and sat down together spectator fashion.

'Oh you'll sort it out,' she replied airily, beginning an exploration of the kitchen drawers. The boys' eyes switched to me, fumbling about with the pages. After a few minutes I got as far as *¿Como se jama usted?* noting that Spain must have Australian printers because all the question marks were upside down. The maid grinned broadly and burst out with *Mi nombre is Marrrrria!* (there was nothing in the book about rolled *r*s), and followed this by a flood of Catalan in which rolled *r*s were sandwiched between lots of words ending in *oss*.

Preparers of phrase books overlook the fact that if you show the slightest tendency to dip your foot into the local lingo pool, it releases a flood in response.

'What did she say?' asked the voice from the kitchen.

'What did she say?' I yelled. 'She said -' I did a rabid impersonation of Maria's collection of rolled *r*s and *osses*!. The kids spluttered giggling into their orange drinks. Even Maria smiled. The duchess took over with her fluent Spanish.

'Look Maria (prods her) you - go (points to door) and come back here (waves to interior) mañana. O.K.?'

'Ah! Si señora. Muchas gracias!'

She went.

'You see,' said the duchess. And that's all she said.

Piqued, my superior intellect challenged by this crude exhibition of sign-language, and in front of my adoring children, I thrust the phrase book firmly into my pocket.

Over the next few days I got to know Mr. Dudley Doust pretty well, phrase-wise that is, and concluded that the compiler was a schizoid manic-depressive, tanked up on the rougher brands of Spanish brandy. Nothing else could account for the Jekyll and Hyde switches in his personality as reflected in the phrases which he had chosen as being vital to the passing tourist. At one moment he was a twitching bag of nerves.

'Do I need a passport for this trip?'
'How deep is it?'
'May I go out?'
'Can you extract it?'
'Does the bus leave on time?'

At the next moment he is a swaggering bully.

'You are occupying my seat!'
'Make out my bill at once!'

'You must wash before you leave!'

Mr Doust thus underwent violent personality changes from a Ms. Hulot to Oberleutenant von Smash of the Waffen S.S.

'Can I sit here?'
'Do you think the carburettor needs cleaning?'
'He ought to be X-rayed!'
'These sheets are dirty!'

Even when he was on the beach Mr. Doust was always looking on the black side:

'Where can we shelter?'
'Is this bay safe for swimming?'
'I think I have sunstroke.'

The coup-de-grâce was, *Tiene usted tarjetas postales de la orbra de pintores de la escuela española?* (Have you any postcards showing the work of the painters of the Spanish school?)

It struck me that with all Dudley Doust's pre-occupations with choked up carburettors, dirty sheets, and wanting his sunstroke X-rayed, his sudden desire to get pictures of paintings of the Spanish school, definitely proved he had lost his Spanish marbles and that overdoses of Carlos 1 brandy had finally got to him. There wasn't one useful phrase like 'Is there any spare crumpet in town?' 'Come on son, where do you eat as opposed to us ripped-off tourists?' In the end I felt sorry for Mr. Doust, he hadn't got one laugh out of his whole experience. I only remember him at all because there was only one phrase in his book which ever came into misuse.

I was enjoying a drink with some friends at a local hotel when the duchess called me from the villa.

'I have to pick up Mildred from the airport,' she explained, 'and I want to tell Maria when she arrives that I'm expecting the baker. Look it up in your phrasebook.'

I rifled through it.

'You don't happen to want your carburettor cleaned or

your dirty sheets changed, do you?' I asked. 'I can give you that.'

'This call is costing us money,' she sing-songed. Suddenly, for no reason at all, I found the phrase she wanted. Good old Dudley. 'It's *Espero la panaderia*,' I informed her.

The scene shifts to the duchess who in the middle of taking a shower and repeating *espero la panaderia* to herself parrot-fashion, suddenly remembered she had left the meringues in the oven. She dashed down in the altogether to remove them. There was a tap on the kitchen door and a young Spaniard entered.

'Oh! Oh! - er - Espero la panaderia,' blurted out the duchess, covering two of her vital parts inadequately with teaspoons. The man grinned and said in perfect English,

'I'm your tour rep. Will I do?'

Helpful Hint

Haven't they got their priorities wrong with air crashes? Shouldn't they put *us* into a black box and to hell with why the plane crashes?

23. Coping with Anno Domini

Rule 1
The formula for combating old age . . . Keep doing what you have done before - it's kept you alive so far.

Rule 2
Old Man (to lady of the town): How about it miss?
   L. of T. (scornfully): You've had it old man!
Old Man: How much do I owe you?

Rule 3
Longevity can be achieved if you don't smoke or drink and live on a vegetarian diet. If you know anyone who followed these rules but died young, it merely means they didn't follow them long enough.

Rule 4
Young man (patronisingly to old lady): I suppose you didn't have the Rolling Stones in your day?
   Old Lady: No, but there was a lot of diphtheria about.

Personal Case History
'Life,' so the saying goes, 'begins at forty.' But I suspect that this is a *bravura* enunciation to cheer up the faint-hearted, for there is little doubt (to those who have passed through it) that life begins its gradual decrescendo after that age.

   Nature is usually kind with the aging process. It's not the sort of thing you can spot in the mirror one morning. You don't usually gaze at your reflection in the mirror and murmur, 'I think I've grown a little older since yesterday'. You can't even tell when you have grown older. (In fact the more you stare at yourself in the mirror the more the reflected image becomes meaningless; a mere blob of flesh which has nothing to do with the inside *you* at all). Again, nature will come to your defence when looking at old snaps or ciné shots of yourself. You don't think 'God! How I've aged since then!' you think 'God! What a callow youth I was then!'

There are those who react to the appearance of their first grey hair as the first sign of growing old: in panic they pull it out or dye it in the vain hope that like Dorian Gray they will remain astonishingly youthful, while the hair in their wedding photograph turns snowy white.

But in my experience the onset of age is far more noticeable in the mental sphere than the physical. At any one point a couple of cells in the cerebellum drop down dead, and you suddenly find that you've lost your enthusiasm for doing the teas for the local cricket club, or turning out at some ungodly hour on a Saturday morning to join the birdwatching society, both of which you have been doing with unalloyed joy for years.

In my own case my musical youth came to a grinding halt when I couldn't enthuse to any pop music after the Beatles. I don't recall going out and buying a single L.P. after that (except old favourites for 25p at a car boot sale). The cut-off was quite dramatic. More brain cells decaying. I really tried to get to like *Led Zeppelin* and *The Moody Blues*, and even some of the later groups whose names seem to parody their own industry like *Ricky Scrotum and the Fallopians* but my brain was saying 'Sorry Guv, they're using a new code, I can't unscramble this lot. Go back to Jack Teagarden, Tommy Dorsey and Beethoven's Fifth.' (It will happen to you!)

Once again nature comes to the rescue. You don't recognise the milestones to Geriatricsville until after you've passed them and look back. You can't spot them coming, and are so spared the horrors of approaching dotage. It wasn't until long afterwards that the duchess and I realised that we had given up going to the cinema.

So if I were asked to describe the difference between life before forty and life after it, I would say it was all the difference (given that the pivotal age of forty is a flexible one) between looking through the windscreen for what is to come, and looking in the rearview mirror at what has gone by.

I've reached the stage when every pub seems to be crowded with 21 year-olds. I find myself wondering in company how many could convert £4.13s. 3½d into new money. The duchess received a blow to her *amour propre* when she let the name Robert Taylor slip out in company and a female frowned and asked 'Who's Robert Taylor?'

'I wouldn't have minded if she had been a young girl,' she said laughingly in spite of herself. 'But she looked at least thirty to me.'

Mercifully, your friends and neighbours, who do notice how old you are getting, refrain from saying so: but you notice they don't greet you so often with a 'My goodness, - you're looking well!'

I could mention other signs of impending decrepitude but I don't wish to depress the reader, and in any case there are compensations. There's always someone in a worse condition than you are. The duchess derives comfort by comparing herself with women approximating her own age and arbitrarily deciding that she looks a damn sight better than they do.

Any suspicion that I was moving towards decay was dispelled the other day when a friend of mine accompanied me into 3 record stores and solemnly asked for a packet of gramophone needles.

Arthur's wife, Cynthia, next door hasn't aged noticeably, she has grown enormously fat instead. Strangers when introduced to her turn very gushing, as if to cover their embarrassment by pretending that fatties are their most favourite people in the world. Privately they are thinking that they need a cicerone to take them on a conducted tour round Cynthia and point out places of historical interest.

Arthur has no complaints. When the subject of age arose over a pint in the psychiatric ward somebody quoted the adage 'you know you're getting old when you begin to notice how young the policemen are looking.'

Arthur smiled ruefully.

'I'm beginning to notice how young everybody's looking - including the old people,' he said. 'But I count myself lucky. According to the theory that every cigarette shortens your life by four minutes, I should have died in 1965.'

Quite a philosopher is Arthur in between puffs.

I am indulging in these sentiments only to remind those on the brink of wedlock, that Time is indeed a fourth dimension in marriage, and when couples have gone through all the active stages of married life, when they have acquired, as Louis McNiece puts it, 'A box to live in with airs and graces. A box on wheels to show its paces', when they have waved farewell to the fledglings as they flee the nest (some flee quicker than others), then they can reap a rich late harvest in their own companionship.

Stay married dear hearts and share the maturing fruits of your autumn. Besides, consider how serviceable folk are to the elderly these days! They run a coach trip to take four of them to the loo. There's bingo, and keep-fit classes, and trips to theatreland; and in winter a trip down to the Costa Brava to fill the empty hotels for a few quid a day. By the time you are fifty you won't be able to wait for your first liver spot and join the Bald Head and Blue Rinse Club. At the very least you have a trusted helpmate to lend a hand with your physical disabilities. The aged wife, I am sure, would much prefer her husband to do up her bra strap when neuralgia strikes, rather than a social worker with cold fingers. And the tottering husband would prefer his wife to give him a kick in the chest if he shows a tendency to keep dying, rather than a mob of paramedics.

In the meantime the duchess and I take each day as it comes. We know we have both failed the computer test:

Question: Do you know how to operate a computer?
Answer: No.
Question: Would you like to learn how to use one?
Answer: No.

which is the modern Rubicon which has to be crossed to obtain citizenship in the coming generation. We are grateful for what sex drive we have, no longer a power generator, more a battery that needs a growing number of days to recharge and produce a spark across our terminals. But our togetherness is a spare tank from which we draw. We lift heavy holiday cases together. On long car journeys we swap the driving duties at regular intervals. We still plan together and hope together and love our grown children together.

'I'm not afraid of dying,' confides the duchess on occasions. 'What annoys me is that when I'm gone I won't know all the things happening to the family and the grandchildren!'

I'm sure she'll find some way of leaving a forwarding address. But neither of us feels any older. Funny thing though, just lately I get the impression that I must be growing taller - when I bend down to pick something up the ground seems farther away . . . and the duchess is of the opinion that there must have been some subsidence in our road - she swears that when she walks up the hill to our house, the hill is steeper than it was . . .

Helpful Hint

Enjoy your advancing years, but don't abuse them. Remember that a little bit of what you fancy makes you limp for a fortnight.

24. The old dog and bone

Rule 1
As soon as your family reaches teenage level, install a payphone.

Rule 2
Here is an interesting question of research. If Alexander Graham Bell was the first man to invent a telephone, whom did he call?

Rule 3
In its counter-measures against obscene phone calls, our phone company has brought out reduced rates for light breathers.

Personal Case History
Most of the marvels of modern technology incorporated into my home have caused no bumps on the highroad of matrimony because they are manifestly either for male or female use. The duchess has no desire to fool around with my chainsaw, my electric drill, or my mini hi-fi system with multi-play compact disc player. (I haven't had much desire to fool around with it either; it would be easier to learn how to fly a spacecraft.) But in a like manner I am very careful not to come within six feet of the duchess's washing machine, blender, or vacuum cleaner. It is only when we come to sharing commonly used installations that dissident voices are heard, such as with the remote control t.v. and V.C.R. machine, when it invariably turns out that I have taped a rugby match over the duchess's carefully recorded Australian soap; which in turn reaches spontaneous combustion levels

when it is discovered that the 9 year old daughter has taped *Star Trek* over them both.

But let us put aside the jangles and clanks of married life for a change and talk about an invention that has proved a benefit to every household, the telephone. Philip Larkin should have written *An Ode to The Old Dog and Bone*. The phone is an instrument of communication, and communication, as Harold Pinter says in some of his plays, is what life is all about; which is remarkable because most of his plays are so obscure, they fail to communicate anything to anybody. But when away from home, I give the old Dutch a ring now and then; it proves to her that the marriage is still working.

In addition to that, the telephone system can be a rich source of humour. Pretty well every householder has at least one telephone story to tell and in my determination to introduce a little light relief, I relate a few true experiences with the telephone passed on to me over the years.

Why is it that so many callers who dial the wrong number refuse to believe they have? You as the victim of the call will no doubt recognise the amusing syndrome as follows:

'Hallo?'

'Hallo, can I speak to Lil please.'

'I'm sorry - you must have the wrong number.'

'Is that - 94360?'

'Yes.'

'Can I speak to Lil please?'

'No. There's no Lil here.'

'Well can you take a message then?'

'No. What I'm trying to say is, if Lil gave you 94360, she gave you the wrong number.'

'Oh... What's her number then?'

'I don't know.

'How d'you know it's the wrong number then?'

'No, listen to me. If Lil gave you 94360, she's given you

my number.'

'Excuse me, who are you?'

'I'm somebody who doesn't know Lil. Look, just check. Has she given you a number and you've dialled it wrongly.'

'The number? It's - 93460.'

'Ah that proves it then. She gave you 93460 and you've dialled 94360. Put the phone down and dial again.'

(VOICE FROM THE LOUNGE) 'Who was that for goodness sake?'

'Don't ask'

RING RING.

'Hallo ?'

'Can I speak to Lil please.'

The instance of the transposed digit causing confusion as exemplified in the little drama above, was likewise the cause of weeks of pain for Albert, a business acquaintance of mine, when he moved into his new house. From 7.00 am onwards on the very first day he received a stream of telephone calls asking what time the next train was for Charing Cross, and following investigation it turned out his number varied but one from the local railway station. The Telephone Manager was sympathetic but regretted that a similar telephone number did not constitute a reason for a re-allocation of a number within the regulations.

Albert immediately thought of revenge and tried to find out the private number of the Telephone Manager so he could transfer his time-table enquiries to him. He might as well have tried to find out the private number of the Queen.

Being of a cynical turn of mind he decided to turn his inconvenience into a private joke, and when anybody called to ask him the time of the next train to Charing Cross, he said any time that came into his head, enjoying a quiet smirk at the thought of all the frowning faces walking up and down the empty platform.

'Sometimes I varied it,' he grinned, 'by asking the caller how far away he was from the station. If he said about twenty minutes, I told him there was one leaving in eighteen minutes and rang off.'

In a final *coup de théâtre* he told every enquirer for a whole week that all trains had been cancelled until further notice.

'No I didn't go down to the station to see what chaos I'd caused,' he concluded. 'I got more pleasure just thinking about it.'

He followed this up by not paying his telephone bill until they changed his number.

That occurred in the days when metropolitan phone numbers were preceded by the abbreviated exchange, requiring one to dial HUR 3672 or CRU 2903, or PAD 6669. Such a combination made them easy to remember and it became a twee suburban custom to boast how many numbers one carried in the head. Enter British Telecom swearing to improve customer service, which they did by introducing 8 and 10 figure numbers which were impossible to remember.

The all-number system produced an even more bizarre instance of wrong dialling than Albert's, which affected Lionel Upper, a member of our rugby club.

At regular intervals Lionel began to receive calls from cafes, restaurants, fairgrounds, and cinemas in the locality, giving bulk orders for Eldorado ice cream. He didn't think much of it at first, assuming that a local depot had opened up with a number similar to his own. But when the hot weather came round he was inundated with panic calls for deliveries.

On this occasion the Telephone Manager was blameless. Following a thorough investigation the manager told Lionel 'There are no manufacturers of ice-cream or storage depots in my district, and the closest phone number to yours is a catholic school in Enders Street.'

So why did the calls pour in? For the time being he left his phone off the hook, particularly if it was a bright sunny morning; but his social and business life began to suffer. 'When one of these calls for delivery come in,' suggested his wife one day, 'why don't you ask them where they get your phone number from?'

What a good idea! It takes a wife to think of sensible solutions like that.

So when the manager of the Regal cinema phoned, Lionel asked him.

'It's on our invoice notes,' the manager replied. 'All deliveries to 66073509.' Now Lionel was getting somewhere. He called Eldorado's Managing Director.

'What's the idea,' he demanded, 'of putting my telephone number on your delivery invoices?' After a pause the reply came back.

'It's not your phone number, it's the map reference of our factory for all our delivery lorries.'

'Well it's the same as my phone number,' roared Lionel. 'And they are all calling me for your ice cream.'

'Why don't you simply change your phone number?' suggested the ice cream king.

'To hell with it,' barked Lionel. 'Move your bloody factory.'

I never heard the sequel because Lionel retired to Seaford shortly after, and didn't say whether or not he bequeathed his burden to the next owner.

'This is Hilary Bannister. I'm sorry I'm not in to receive your call. If you would like to leave your name and number, I will call you back as soon as possible. Please speak after the tone . . .'

Well of course, they rarely do ring you back, and this relatively new B.T. toy costs you 50p to leave a message. The answer-phone is just one of the technological necessities which aren't necessities at all. Everyone swears they hate them, but more and more are buying them. As we grow older,

I sense, the fewer and more pedestrian are the nature of our incoming calls, and I see no reason why I should invest in expensive equipment just to suffer the embarrassment of returning home, switching on the machine, and being greeted by recorded silence.

I am usually caught hopping on making outgoing calls, having to deliver a message immediately after a blip; my recording must come over to the listener like: 'Ah! Er! Shum flmm makk - er - izzat er no - er -' before I start to make sense.

The tape does occasionally run out too, or people gabble immediately and long before the tone, so that half the message is lost. This brings me to my last true anecdote which concerned a member of our golf club, who switched on his answerphone to hear a frantic female, who must have committed the error in her panic of not waiting for the tone, and all he heard was '... and he's died in the bath and I don't know what to do!' So short and hysterical was the *cri-de-coeur*, he couldn't even identify the voice.

Over the next five minutes he called everyone on his list of his relatives and close friends to see if anyone of them had been bereft of a partner in the bath . . .

'Is that you Mildred? Is Jack there?'

'No, he's having a bath.'

'He's not dead is he?'

'Dead? Don't scare me like that. I hope he's not dead, he's still singing.'

'Somebody phoned on my machine and said that someone had died in the bath.'

'Who died in the bath?'

'That's what I'm trying to find out. She was in such a panic I couldn't recognise her voice and she didn't say her name.'

'Shall I phone Kath? You know Fred's on the borderline don't you.'

'You phone Kath, and Margaret and Joan, and I'll phone the Bennets and the Palmers . . .'

'I'd better run up and take a look at Jack first, he's suddenly stopped singing.'

'Don't be daft Mildred. The woman on the phone had already found her corpse, I'm not looking for more.'

The cycle of calls having been made, no reports came in of anyone struggling to get a recent departed out of the tub. My friend was forced to turn his mind to that larger amorphous body of social acquaintances with whom he was not on personal intimate terms, but who might call him in an emergency. Of these, he tried to recollect those whose lives were on the blink and wobble. This took him another hour and put another £10 on his phone bill. No dead bodies in the bath. Mildred called back.

'So many people know by now, you'd think that if it was anyone near, somebody would have heard about it.'

Another hour went by, with our hero making the odd calls to anyone he could recall not looking too well on the last occasion of meeting him, but with no result. By now it occurred to him that even if he traced the bereaved victim, it would be too late to render any assistance, and he gave up in despair. Perhaps it was a crossed line, which might explain the fragmentary nature of the message.

Over the next few weeks he was sporadically nagged by the unsolved problem. On visiting other people's homes, he found himself taking a surreptitious look into the bathroom, which he admitted had no logical reasoning behind it because the husbands were all alive and kicking. On the other hand the voice had only said *he* and it could have been a brother or a son, or a lover. After a time, he dismissed it altogether from his mind and eventually forgot about it.

Nearly a year later he was slaking his thirst at the 19th hole and the subject of conversation got round to membership.

'I've only been a member for a year or so,' put in my friend, 'and I find it difficult to get to know peoples' names. After all, there are over three hundred members all playing golf . . .'

'Pity about old what's-his-name,' said one.

'Who's-his-name?'

'I can't remember, because he died the day he joined. He was five years on the waiting list, and the day he finally got in, he popped it. Played his first game, went home, and died in the bath.'

'Died in the bath?' spluttered my friend, spraying expensive gin and tonic.

'Apparently his wife didn't know a soul - one of those timid domesticites you know - and phoned up everybody she could find in his brand new membership card. About a dozen fellers turned up and got him out of the bath.'

'Oh well,' said another, 'at least he got his game of golf in first. Half a loaf is better than none.'

Half a loaf possibly, thought my friend ruefully, but not half a telephone message.

Helpful Hint

To conclude on another little true story.

Little Lucy was determined to ring up Father Christmas personally and tell him what she wanted for Christmas. Her father called a friend and asked him to pretend to be Santa when he got Lucy to ring back. The friend waited and the phone duly rang.

'Ho Ho Ho!' he boomed. 'This is Father Christmas speaking.'

'Well this is Mrs. Christmas,' said a voice. 'Get your sledge out, the bloody car has broken down.'

25. Madness

'So you're getting married?' I opened up with my godson, as I eased into my usual niche in the *Anchor and Hope*. (It was just an odd circumstance that I had never been asked to be a Best Man, but I was godfather to so many friends' offspring I qualified for the Mafia).

'In that case,' I pursued, 'remember that all women are mad.'

'Mad?'

'Well they are all perverse, paranoiac, peevish, illogical, moody, contrary, live on a knife edge between gushing and pique, short on forgiveness, long on grudge, wayward, vacillating, prick-teasing, and are motivated more by fantasy than reality. So it's much simpler to call them mad - especially the last bit because madness after all is a confusion between fantasy and reality.'

'You're not trying to put me off marriage by any chance?'

'On the contrary. You're about to embark on a wonderful adventure which no other institution can provide - as long as you remember you are about to share a life with a mental case.'

'From a man's point of view . . .'

'Is there another one? As the pretty girl said to Max Beerbohm - "After all, women are a sex by themselves so to speak". You don't so much share a life with them, you sort of - live alongside ' em. By the way, mine's a gin and tonic - you're not getting this advice for nothing.'

The young man grinned condescendingly.

'You're not actually saying that all women are lunatics and think they are Napoleon?'

'No, it's the husbands who often end up by thinking their wives are Napoleon. To put it into your jargon, all women are a few bites short of a floppy disc. Cheers!'

'Cheers...'

'Let's get down to specifics. Has your beloved - while you were busy exploring her body on the sofa - said in a teasing sort of way, "You men are all the same - you're only after one thing!"'

He looked a bit sheepish.

'Well, I suppose she has.'

'That's the first sign of madness. Can you imagine a doe turning round to a stag in the rutting season and saying, "All you stags are the same, you're only after one thing"? Can you see a porcupine sneering at her mate, "You only want me for my body"? Of course not! The female is after the same thing as the male, but only women pretend they're not. Madness.'

'So what's the answer to that one?'

'The next time she accuses you of only being after one thing, say "If you've got two, I'll go after that one as well."'

'That might make her laugh.'

'All the better, it'll make her breasts heave - very exciting. I suppose you've already said to her on occasions, "You're looking very beautiful tonight darling"?'

'Quite a few times, yes.'

'What does she say?'

'She sort of blushes - and says "thank you darling".'

'She won't say that after you're married.'

'What will she say?'

'She'll say "If you think you're playing golf tomorrow you're mistaken".'

'Why would she say that?'

'You'll find out. Does she sometimes say, "Do you love me darling?"'

'All the time.'

'She's not deaf is she?'

'Deaf? Of course not.'

'Then why does she keep asking?'
'It's - it's - just a little endearment that's all.'
'She doesn't think you're going to change your mind since the last time she asked?'
'No. I wouldn't change my mind about that sort of thing.'
'You're not likely to say, "I loved you an hour ago, but I'm starting to go off you a bit"?'
'No.'
'Are you sure about that?'
'Of course I'm - look, this whole line of questioning is mad.'
'Exactly what I'm trying to prove. She keeps asking because she's mad.' I indicated that my glass needed refilling. 'She'll ask you the same question after you're married of course. "Do you love me?" But when you say, "Of course I do darling," her answer will be different.'
'What will she say?'
'She'll pout a little and say, "You're only saying that!"'
'You're only saying that?'
'No, "You're only *saying* that".'
'Why would she say that?'
'Because.'
'Because?'
'Yes. You'll get that answer a lot of times. When you ask why it's always you who has to take out the trash, or tell the kids off, or complain about something to the next door neighbour, she'll say, "Because".'
'Because what?'
'Because nothing. Here am I trying to prove all women are mad and you keep ignoring the evidence.'
'Frankly I'm confused.'
'Good. That's the first sign of understanding women. So let's see what your chances are. Tell me something, in the whole spectrum between women being soft cuddly bundles who dote on your every word, and Genghis Khans wielding

a whip, where does your fiancée stand?'

'She relies on me for everything.'

'You mean she's all goo-goo eyed, and asks things like "Does this lipstick suit me sweetheart? What dress shall I wear? Would you like my hair short?"'

'Er - she hasn't actually asked me about her hair.'

'No sign of bossiness at all? She doesn't flick a little scurf off your suit, or straighten your tie, or push your fringe back if it flops forward?'

'No.'

'She hasn't even started to make coy little concessions like, "You don't have to come over and see me tomorrow darling if you don't want to. I shall understand." Because that really means, "You'd better come over and see me tomorrow or I'll want to know why".'

'No, she doesn't say that sort of thing as far as I remember.'

'By heck - she is bottling it up.'

'Bottling it up?'

'She's got you flying at 20,000 feet - giving you the impression that you're her god and she's going to worship you from here on in. But that's just the bait before she strikes with the grappling hook.'

'Grappling hook?'

'She's going to slap you on the slab like a stuck flounder and really go to work on you, because you'll have no resistance - one minute you're a god and the next you're a walking-talking robot.'

My godson took a greedy gulp of his beer.

'You're not seriously maintaining that all women want their husbands to be walking-talking robots?'

'No, that's a second choice. The first choice is to have no husband at all. Get pregnant and a council house and raise a family on their own.' He sighed and nodded.

'Even I don't understand all that single mothers crap.

They can't hate men that much. What about love and romance and simple physical pleasures?'

'Oh they enjoy all that in the abstract in Mills and Boon, and Barbara Cartland, and in endless soaps, but they would hate it to happen to them.'

'So you're saying that women are capricious and unpredictable, because they are constantly at odds with their romantic fantasies and reality? But that doesn't make them mad does it?'

'Well - they're always mad at something! But choose your own epithet for a sex who pays out a £1000 for a wedding dress she will only wear once, but then will drive ten miles to a garage to save a £1 on cheaper petrol, which takes £2 of petrol to get there.

'Who looks at her wardrobe so crammed with clothes that even the moths haven't learned to fly, and says "I haven't got a thing to wear."

'Who watches Delia Smith make cakes and religiously writes down the recipes, and then buys ready-made ones at Sainsbury's. Who asks you to write letters of complaint because she says you are so much better at that sort of thing, and then leans over your shoulder and tells you exactly what to write.

'Who yelps "Rubbish" at t.v. ads which claim their face cream reduces wrinkles, and then goes out and buys a large pot of it. Who never gets to cook anything in her deep-freeze because she never remembers to take it out and defrost it in time for the meal.

'Who can happily join a "Women are Not Sex Objects" demonstration on her way to an aerobics class and a beauty treatment. Who never misses that annual lunch with her oldest and dearest and sole-surviving schoolfriend, and assassinates her character as soon as she leaves. Who, once she has really made up her mind, changes it. Who never lets the word "risk" enter her vocabulary.

'Who, despite several millennia since Eve, can't spot a snake-in-the-grass, and whose steel casing melts into a wad of malleable putty under the spell of a charming cad. Who wakes you up in the middle of the night and says, "I can't sleep, can you?"

'And who insists that as a married couple you shouldn't keep any secrets from each other, largely because she hasn't got any, and it's bullets in her gun if you have, and are fool enough to tell them.'

'So if all women aren't mad, what would you call them?'

My godson thought for a minute.

'Opposite, I'd say,' he grinned. "After all, they're not called the opposite sex for nothing.'

'I'll settle for that,' I said.

'Did you say all this to your last godson?' he asked.

'Of course. He joined the Foreign Legion. But there's not much difference between marriage and the Foreign Legion. Both involve being locked up in a fort, surrounded by hostile tribes, and ruled by a tyrannical Commandant.'

'You're kidding of course.'

'Just testing you. You'll need a sense of humour. So drink up.'

'What's the rush?' He glanced at his watch. 'The women said lunch will be between one o'clock and half past.'

'Which means that if we're not there by a quarter to one we'll be on a charge. Haven't you learned anything?'

It's just as well I'm nearly down to my last godson.

26. The night they invented sex

As distinct from the night they invented Champagne, for example, as celebrated in the *Gigi* song, because They - the Heavenly Host, or whatever - must have sat down one night and invented sex as a way of reproducing the human (and animal) species, and considering how much trouble it has caused, one wonders how a bunch of superior beings could have picked on it. I imagined a sort of Board Meeting in the sky of this Universal Conglomerate, and how they came to this decision.

The Chairman banged his gavel.

'To order gentlemen. As you know the Big Chief has decided to proceed with his project *Human Race* and is relying on us to devise a method of continually reproducing itself so that it doesn't expire.'

A hand was raised.

'Ah - St Cuthbert of the philosophy department. Yes?'

'Why are we giving ourselves this headache, Mr. Chairman, of reproducing the species? Why don't we give this new race everlasting life?'

'Cuthie baby,' sighed the Chairman. 'Haven't you read the Big Chief's prospectus on this subject? He doesn't want humans to be as perfect as us. He wants them to struggle towards perfection, generation by generation, by believing in his good works.'

'Oh well - if you're going to bring religion into it,' dismissed St. Cuthbert.

The Chairman scribbled a note on his pad. *St.Cuth. Four extra days harping*, and then addressed two distinguished gentlemen at the end of the table.

'Er Seraphims Fusch and Polanski of the physiology

department, I gather you have already made considerable progress in this direction?'

The two rose, smiling smugly.

'Mr. Chairman,' announced Fusch smoothly. 'We have virtually solved the whole problem of the reproduction of the human race at regular intervals and would like to present our programme before the Board.'

'I'm glad that some people are not wasting their time up here.' grunted the Chairman, throwing a dagger look at St. Cuthbert. 'Proceed Seraphim Fusch.'

That worthy pressed a button and took up some notes.

'We have divided the human race into two sexes: male and female . . .'

At this point a man and a woman in their naked innocence entered the room.

'The one on the left is the female and the one on the right is male. These are just laboratory mock-ups you understand, gentlemen, for the purposes of demonstration. We don't pretend to be so clever as the Big Chief.'

'Crawler,' muttered St. Cuthbert, and earned another glare from the Chairman.

'The race will be perpetuated by a copulative act between the two species which results in the implantation of the newly-born inside the body of the female, which she eventually delivers.'

'I've never heard of a more crude and messy idea,' cried St. Cuthbert. 'And why burden the female with all that trouble?'

'Shut up Cuthbert,' hissed the Chairman.

Fusch, unmoved, turned to his colleague.

'Please demonstrate, Polanski.'

Polanski took up an electronic gizmo and operated some buttons.

'The pair have now been programmed to perform the copulative procedure . . .'

The members of the Board all leaned forward and gazed with dispassionate interest.

'You will observe,' continued Polanski, 'that the two bodies have engaged in a certain area, allowing an impregnating fluid to pass from the male to the female and in doing so . . .' Polanski's voice droned on . . . 'And that completes the reproductive act.'

There was a long silence while Polanski programmed the robot man and woman to exit.

'But where is the newly produced human being?' asked a voice.

Fusch turned with an impatient glint in his eye.

'I have already explained, it exists in embryo form inside the female, which she will eventually deliver.'

'How long does that take?'

'We have planned about nine months.'

'In that case, what was all that rush at the end?'

'Yes,' queried the Chairman. 'They did seem at the end of that performance to be somewhat in a hurry to get it over with, Fusch. It seemed to knock the stuffing out of both of them. All that panting and sweating. I mean, if they won't *like* doing it, bang goes your next generation.'

It was Polanski's turn to rise with an impatient glint in his eye.

'I assure you, Mr. Chairman, the bodies of the two sexes will be programmed to experience up to level 6 on our *Ecstasy Scale* at the culmination of the act. It won't be a question of their not liking to do it, they will be chewing their way through doors to do it.'

'Level 6?' drawled a voice. 'That's a damn sight too good for them.'

'Then choose your own level,' snarled Polanski, taking his seat.

'Views gentlemen?' asked the Chairman smoothly.

An eccentric bearded worthy rose angrily to his feet.

'Views, Mr. Chairman? Views? My department doesn't need views. We have facts. We have put Polanksi and Fusch's project through our predictive computer programme and it spells disaster. Nothing could be more messy, time-and-money-wasting, and embarrassing to the human race than sex. At worst it will lead to schoolboys hiding grubby sex books inside their school primers. To grown men skulking round strip joints; to video nasties and porno centres; to the pill and the condom. At best, even at its very best Mr. Chairman, sex will occupy half the life of every male and female, addictive votaries at the altar of the Orgasm. And just think of all the agonies of dissimulation the ordinary decent male has to go through to attract a female and restart the human race? Swearing eternal love and fidelity; buying her flowers and presents; taking tea with her parents and pretending he's twice as nice as he actually is; fumbling with her underwear in the car, scheming dirty weekends in Brighton. Is that really the best that Heaven can come up with as a way to perpetuate the human race? Frankly the whole system is murky, riddled with taboos, not to mention diseases, and in my view stinks.'

'Hear hear.'

'Shut up, St. Cuthbert,' said the Chairman. 'Who are you, sir, anyway?'

'I'm St. Convolvulus,' replied the eccentric, 'of the Flower Department. And we have already perfected a system of regenerating the system with pollen.'

'With pollen?'

'Yes. The bees deposit the pollen from one flower on to another and that cross pollination creates a new flower. Now I see no reason why we can't adopt that method with humans, except we use dandruff. In one fell swoop we'll do away with whorehouses, sex shops, and vice squads...'

'A bit - sort of chemical, isn't it?' sniffed Polanski.

'I'm on his side for a change,' said St. Cuthbert. 'If I were one his males, I wouldn't get much kick out of knowing my dandruff had been mixed up by a bee with the dandruff scraped off some dolly fixture.'

'What's a dolly fixture?' asked St. Convolvulus.

'I dunno - one of those you hit Level 6 with, I guess.'

A young man sprang to his feet.

'I feel there's a case of industrial espionage here. We in the botanical department have already perfected a propagation method with trees and plants. Send in that male thing again.'

The male prototype was eventually reintroduced.

'Now,' he continued, producing a pair of secateurs and a pot of earth. 'We don't need that female contraption. We just cut a bit off the man here. Say just above the knuckle.' He neatly chopped off a finger. 'Stick in the pot with a bit of hormone powder, and in time we just grow a new human. What's wrong with that? No pills, no condoms, no grubby sex aberrations either.'

Polanski gave a nasty laugh.

'And he's stuck in a pot forever, you numbskull! How can he possibly move about with his feet rooted in a pot?'

'Why does he want to move about? One place is the same as another?'

'Why make him in the first place then?' snarled Polanski.

'Order gentlemen, please,' cried the Chairman. 'Remember where we are.'

'As head of the Marine Biology department,' said another, 'we have with one species that has done away with sex as such. For example the oyster is strictly a bi-valve. One moment it is female and the next moment a male, so getting the best of both worlds.'

'That's no good,' said St. Cuthbert. 'A male would get up to give his seat in the bus to a lady, and by the time she sat down, she would be a man and he would be a lady, and they'd spend all day getting up and down.'

'Why can't humans be like oak trees?' suggested another bright spark. 'Instead of dropping acorns, they could drop their noses; or something,' he ended lamely.

A general argument broke out and the Chairman banged his gavel.

'Come, come now gentlemen. Oak trees, bi-valves, cross-pollination - there are a thousand ways of reduplicating an original model species, but we don't want anything purely mechanical. Don't forget the Big Chief has insisted these humans must have a free will and a choice between good and evil.'

'What's evil?' called a voice.

'We don't know yet, but the general consensus of opinion is that humans given a choice are bound to screw themselves up in the end, and that's why I favour the Fusch-Polanski method.'

Loud groans.

'No, no,' insisted the Chairman, 'the sexual method as demonstrated by our colleagues could be the method widest open to abuse, and so provide that very open field of choice which the Big Chief is after. Any questions?'

'Before the questions,' said Polanski, 'I should say in this very intimate act, there are rules of propriety, etiquette, and moral principles which the consenting sexes must adhere to, with built-in deterrents if they don't.'

'What are they?' asked a voice.

'We call them sexually transmitted diseases or a dose of the clap.'

'What about animals?' called another. 'I see the Big Chief is also starting an animal kingdom, birds, insects, and beasts.'

'They will be programmed in the same method,' said Polanski smoothly. 'But more instinctive. We have calculated that animals are more in danger of becoming extinct, so their urge to breed will be made more powerful and less sophisticated. I mean there may come a time when we simply can't afford to have lesbian elephants and faggot tigers.'

'May we have a show of wings for the sex method please?' prompted the Chairman. There was a counting.

'Against? ... Aren't you for *anything* St. Cuthbert?'

'I'm all for the human race but I don't call this a democracy. They're not even here to vote, poor bastards.'

27. Residual guides to married life

Don't marry a woman who says she is a light eater. You'll find that as soon as it's light, she eats.

Teach a nubile daughter by all means the old Christian precept that 'you can't take it with you', but that doesn't mean she should start to give it away early.

If your wife drops those dreaded words 'We must have a spare room for when mother stays', decorate the walls with travel posters.

If she must have a deep freeze, buy a small one. Otherwise she will be asking 'What do you want for dinner on January 21st next year?'

If your wife or children go on a plane flight, tell them to sit in the rear. Planes seldom crash backwards into mountains.

If you plan to have a large family, make sure it isn't the wife's.

Don't marry a girl who makes out she has already been asked to marry half a dozen times. Five of them are asked by her mother and father.

Value kids for what they are. They are the only ones who know how to undo child-proof bottles of aspirins when you've got a splitting headache.

Discourage your daughter from wearing skirts which will give her chapped buttocks, and your son from wearing jeans making him liable to arrest for indecent enclosure.

Face sexual realities. If all the school virgins were laid end to end, you shouldn't be at all surprised.

Remember your wife will try to reform you on the basis that if they can make penicillin out of mouldy bread, she can make something out of you.

Don't boast too much to the young'uns about 'the good old days.' Just point out that it used to take a lot more onions to smarm over a piece of steak, and let them work it out.

Teach your kids independence. Tell them that if they ever need a helping hand, there's one at the end of their arm.

Epilogue

What sort of marriage would sir and madam prefer?

The duchess read my finished efforts with some reluctance as she was in the middle of crocheting 480 squares which she said would make a tablecloth or a bed-cover when sewn together, but which I said would make a big top for a circus.

'The point is,' she observed, putting down the book and picking up her needles in one smooth movement, 'there isn't a single law of the land which protects marriage as an institution these days - in fact with all these hand-outs it gives to unmarried mothers, couples living together and kids born out of wedlock, it's doing its best to get rid of it. Look at Norma Nesbitt...'

I had looked at Norma Nesbitt often. She was a dishy piece of goods and quite a number of males had looked at Norma, because Norma *slept around*. Eventually she had a baby and the father refused to marry her. The event caused a family furore. Although it happened in the Nesbitt house at the bottom of the street, the details were soon well known to the houses at the top of the street with a rapidity that outpaced the town gossip Peggy Cartwright. It so happened that Norma's kin were all of the old school, and refused to be melted by Norma's little white bundle.

'And how do you propose to bring him up?' demanded an outraged aunt.

'Oh I get a state allowance, don't I,' smiled Norma.

'Which we have to pay for!' said the aunt turning white with rage. 'Why should I pay for you to lie on your back for anybody that comes along in trousers? I have no sympathy for you and neither does George!'

George said he didn't have any sympathy for her either. And another aunt said,

'And I suppose if you go out to work, you're going to

dump the child on your mother?'

And she did go out to work and she did off-load the white bundle on to mum.

'Bigamy,' I said at last. 'That's one law which protects the institution of marriage - in a sort of way.'

'Fat lot of good that is,' dismissed the duchess.

Yes, it was a fat lot of good. I secretly admired bigamists - not the for their morals but for their sheer energy. Any husband that has brought up a family can only stand aghast at a man who doubles the burden and seems to derive some pleasure out of it. And here such laws on marriage as there were had taken on a dichotomy, for whereas it shows no interest in an unmarried man who fathers children all over the place and absconds, it is relentless in its pursuit of married men who do the same.

'More fool you for getting married!' the law says. 'If you had stayed single you would have got away with it.' And a mote of pity for the bigamist: a young buck can shack up with as many birds as he likes, and father as many children, but if a married man takes on two wives at once he is sent down as a dirty rotter. Although suffering from a feeling of *déja-vu*, I saw the duchess's protest in greater depth.

'It's spine-chilling,' she went on, a wisp of smoke arising from her enmeshing needles. 'How can you advise a daughter to do the right thing when she says, "What do I want to get married for? It's only a slip of paper?"'

'Good God!' I exclaimed. 'Have I been held to you all these years by only a slip of paper?'

She threw me a look.

'If you want to know the answer to that these days the answer is *yes*. Didn't you read the paper yesterday? Women go into these sperm banks and as soon as they become pregnant they give her an allowance and a council house. It's absolutely mind boggling. What's happening to the world we were brought up in? No wonder the Norma Nesbitt's go around all cocksure and arrogant. I'll tell you, the only reason why girls get married these days is because they want a church wedding and to wear white.'

'Well at least the church has got something going for it,' I said. 'They should capitalise on that.'

'The church!' scoffed she. 'What can they do? They can't make laws.'

'No, but as you say,' I pursued, 'the church wedding is a big pull, so why don't they offer church weddings to anybody, whether they get married or not?'

She gave me an old-fashioned look.

'There would be nothing illegal about it, because as you said, nobody gets prosecuted these days for living together and raising a family. It would be a way for them to bring all the rebels into the fold.'

I pursued the whimsy of being a whiz-kid marketing manager hired by the Ecumenical Council to come up with an attractive colour brochure . . .

Custom-made Wedding Ceremonies to suit your personal needs! Are you a female careerist or an active Women's-Libber who either is already, or plans to be a single parent? Why not get married to yourself in our specially adapted *Single Persons Marriage Ceremony*? Enjoy the extra thrill of having your daughters as your bridesmaids!

Are you raising a family with a 'live-in' boyfriend, but have always hankered after a church wedding? Enjoy our special *Non-Marriage Ceremony*! We offer a full wedding ceremony with organ, choir, solemnisation and exchange of rings, only stopping short of joining you as man and wife. Go away having enjoyed the full glamour of a wedding but still free to leave each other whenever you feel like it!

Our *Kwik Multi-Marriage Ceremony* caters for those who like to amass as many wives or husbands as they can. (Especially for fading show-biz personalities who seek the publicity). Our carefully worded wedding ceremony ('for richer for poorer, for better or worse, but for an optional 30 days only . . .') allows you to swap partners every month legally without divorce. Ladies! Outdo Elizabeth Taylor and have 12 new husbands in a year!

Our *Gay and Lesbian Service* is directly taken from the Holy Mackerel Church of St. Rutch of the State of Winsconsin who pioneered the ceremony. (Please state beforehand which one is the bride. He or she may wear white.)

As much as I have pitied myself over these pages, I feel greater pity for those who think they have outsmarted the system. O.K. so marriage involves a huge sacrifice, equally on the part of the woman as the man. But like all things in life, the richness of the reward is greater than the pain. And those who try to enter the contract with a built-in cop-out will never really enjoy the ecstatic agony of a relationship. For me, the duchess and my children are those for whom I would happily and willingly lay down my life. The wisdom of ages is not easily gainsayed.